THE BIG BOOK OF SALADS

THE BIG BOOK OF SALADS

Your complete guide to creating perfect salads every time

LOVE FOOD™

First published in 2010
LOVE FOOD is an imprint of Parragon Books Ltd

Parragon
Queen Street House
4 Queen Street
Bath BA1 1HE, UK

ISBN: 978-1-4075-8819-3

Printed in China

Internal design by Simon Levy
New photography by Clive Bozzard-Hill
New home economy by Valerie Barrett
New recipes, introduction and cover text by Angela Drake

Notes for the Reader

This book uses both metric and imperial measurements. Follow the same units of measurement throughout; do not mix metric and imperial. All spoon measurements are level: teaspoons are assumed to be 5 ml, and tablespoons are assumed to be 15 ml. Unless otherwise stated, milk is assumed to be full fat, eggs and individual vegetables are medium, and pepper is freshly ground black pepper.

The times given are an approximate guide only. Preparation times differ according to the techniques used by different people and the cooking times may also vary from those given. Optional ingredients, variations or serving suggestions have not been included in the calculations.

Recipes using raw or very lightly cooked eggs should be avoided by infants, the elderly, pregnant women, convalescents and anyone suffering from an illness. Pregnant and breastfeeding women are advised to avoid eating peanuts and peanut products. Sufferers from nut allergies should be aware that some of the ready-made ingredients used in the recipes in this book may contain nuts. Always check the packaging before use.

Vegetarians should be aware that some of the ready-made ingredients used in the recipes in this book may contain animal products. Always check the packaging before use.

The publisher would like to thank Getty images for the permission to reproduce the front cover image.

CONTENTS

INTRODUCTION

FULL OF GOODNESS

Gone are the days when the word 'salad' conjured up the image of a few limp lettuce leaves on the side of your plate. Salads have really come of age with the most vibrant and exciting range of ingredients available to create sensational dishes to suit any occasion.

A quick stroll around even the smallest supermarket or greengrocer will reveal a cornucopia of fantastic salad ingredients, from peppery salad leaves and fragrant herbs to colourful sun-ripened fruit and vegetables – so easy to transform into fresh and appetizing meals with minimum time and effort. Today, salads are the most versatile of dishes incorporating flavours from all around the world. Whether it's a traditional crisp Greek salad, a filling warm chicken and pasta salad or an energy boosting bean salad, you'll find the perfect salad to feed family and friends.

THE HEALTHY OPTION

The health benefits of regularly eating salads cannot be ignored. We all aspire to living a healthier lifestyle and eating salads packed with nutritious leafy greens, vegetables, pulses, herbs, nuts and seeds, will certainly boost your intake of protein and essential vitamins, minerals and fibre. We are frequently reminded that a healthy diet includes eating a minimum of five portions of fruit and vegetables every day – tuck into a hearty salad for lunch or dinner or replace rice or potatoes with a tasty side salad and you will be well on the way to that target.

For those who are constantly having to watch their weight this book will be a revelation. Not long ago anyone on a diet would stick to a simple, but very boring, virtually calorie-free salad of lettuce, tomato, cucumber and celery with no dressing! Well, times have certainly changed. Choose carefully and you can still enjoy a thoroughly satisfying salad without piling on the pounds. Look out for salads that have yogurt-based dressings such as Sweet Potato Salad or ones that are only lightly dressed such as Wild Rice Salad with Cucumber & Orange or Minted Pea & Melon Salad.

However, don't be put off by the quantity of oil in many of the dressings. A healthy balanced diet needs to include a small amount of fat. Nut and vegetable oils (such as sunflower and olive oil) contain unsaturated fat which can help to lower harmful cholesterol in the blood. Also, the fat in

some oils and oily fish, such as mackerel, contains the essential omega-3 or omega-6 fatty acids that are important for growth, healthy skin and a strong immune system.

Grains, pulses and beans play an important role in a healthy diet and can release a steady supply of energy throughout the day. On hectic and energetic days pick a fibre-packed salad such as Three Bean or Tabbouleh for lunch and you'll find that hunger pangs are kept well at bay for a good few hours.

A SALAD FOR ALL SEASONS

It's not surprising that many of us only think about eating or cooking salads during the summer – salads are the perfect solution for easy to prepare meals when the days are long and hot. But salads really can be served all year round and in this book you'll find salads to suit all times of year, whatever the weather. We are no longer restricted by seasonal fluctuations for many ingredients and fresh produce can be flown all over the world. Let's face it, nothing can beat the flavour of freshly dug new potatoes in a delicious creamy dressed potato salad – the ideal accompaniment for a sizzling summer barbecue or alfresco supper.

Springtime is one of the best times of the year for serving salads. Shops will be full to the brim with an abundance of crisp young spring vegetables and seasonal salad leaves. With days becoming longer and warmer, light and nutritious salads are the natural choices to boost our energy levels after the winter slump.

In the heat of summer, choose salads that are quick and easy to cook – no one wants to be working away in a hot kitchen when they could be outdoors enjoying the good weather. For alfresco dinner parties, summer buffets and barbecues, pick salads that can be made a few hours in advance or prepare the separate elements of the salads and simply toss together just before serving.

During the colder months of the year, opt for comforting and hearty warm salads or filling pasta or rice salads. Take time to marinate fish, meat and poultry for extra flavour or slow roast vegetables with winter herbs and garlic. If you're entertaining, a salad can be the ideal light starter choice for a winter dinner party.

THE FINEST INGREDIENTS

Never before has there been such a huge range of salad ingredients to choose from. Here's a quick guide to some of the essentials.

SALAD LEAVES

With an endless variety of shapes, textures, colour and flavour, salad leaves really do make or break a good salad. Leaves with a robust and peppery taste include curly endive (also called frisée), rocket, mizuna and watercress. For a salad with a milder taste, pick delicate lamb's lettuce or a classic round butterhead. For the crispiest salad you can't beat cos or iceberg lettuces. To add extra colour to a leafy salad, look out for chard leaves with ruby red stalks, variegated oak leaf or lollo rosso leaves or firm red chicory leaves.

Many of the recipes in this book suggest using bags of mixed salad leaves and you'll find an ever-changing selection of leafy mixtures in most supermarkets. Quick to buy and very convenient, they are a boon to the busy cook. However, do check them for freshness as the leaves can deteriorate quite quickly. Don't worry if you can't find a specific salad bag for a recipe – simply substitute another one or buy separate leaves and make up your own mix.

HERBS

Fragrant fresh herbs can bring an everyday salad to life. The classic Mediterranean herbs such as basil, oregano and flat-leaf parsley are essentials for many salads and go particularly well with tomatoes, peppers and onions. Coriander and mint add an aromatic touch to Asian and Middle Eastern themed salads, while delicate and feathery herbs such as dill, fennel and chervil with their mild aniseed taste, suit fish and seafood salads. More robust herbs with woody stalks such as thyme and rosemary are great for adding to marinades – simply bruise or break the stalks to release more flavour.

If you have space in the garden it's worth growing your own herbs or planting a few in a window box or hanging basket for handy picking. Alternatively, buy pots of growing herbs and pop them in a shaded spot on the kitchen windowsill and remember to water them regularly.

OILS

The basis of most salad dressings, the choice of good quality oil is vital to a successful salad. Extracted from various nuts, seeds and beans, oils can vary in flavour from bland and virtually tasteless to highly aromatic and intensely rich.

Olive oil is by far the most popular oil to use in most dressings. Produced in hot Mediterranean countries such as France, Greece, Italy and Spain, the prized extra virgin olive oil is considered the finest. It has a dark green colour and strong rich taste and is from the first cold pressing of olives. Use sparingly as it can be overpowering for some delicate salads. Milder and paler olive oils from further pressings may be more suitable for some recipes.

Nut oils can also vary considerably in flavour and intensity. Groundnut oil (also called peanut oil) is a pale oil with a mild and nutty aroma. Walnut and hazelnut oils have wonderfully intense flavours but they can be quite pricey. Buy in small quantities and use within a few months of opening as they can soon go rancid.

Sesame seed oil is frequently used in oriental themed salads. It has a deep amber colour and a heady aroma with a really nutty taste. A few drops are all that's needed for most recipes.

Sunflower and corn oil both have a fairly mild, somewhat bland taste. Use them for dressings and marinades where other stronger flavourings will dominate such as fresh herbs, garlic or chilli. They can also be blended with more expensive oils to dilute the intense flavour.

VINEGARS

The second essential element of a salad dressing is usually vinegar. Those distilled from wine – either white or red – are the most frequently used in salad dressings. Other vinegars such as sherry and cider are popular too and can be used to compliment the ingredients in a salad. Mild and sweet cider vinegar goes particularly well with salads that contain fruit while rich and nutty sherry vinegar is delicious with warm meat and poultry salads.

Balsamic vinegar comes from the Italian region of Modena and is a rich, yet mellow vinegar that has a wonderfully sweet and sour flavour. Just like the finest olive oils it can be very expensive. The vinegar is aged in oak casks between five and twenty years – the longer the ageing process the higher the price. It's delicious used on its own to simply dress sliced ripe tomatoes or roasted vegetable salads or try simmering it with a little sugar to make a divine syrupy balsamic glaze for drizzling over sweet or savoury salads.

SEEDS & NUTS

A sprinkling of crunchy nuts or seeds can add plenty of extra interest to salads as well as boosting your intake of protein, essential vitamins and minerals. Keep small quantities of pumpkin, sunflower and sesame seeds as well as a selection of unsalted nuts in the storecupboard. To bring out more of their flavour, lightly toast nuts and seeds by spreading on a baking sheet and popping under a hot grill for a few minutes.

BEANS, PASTA & RICE

These great energy foods can form the basis of really substantial and filling salads. Although most have a fairly bland flavour on their own, the addition of herbs, spices and dressings can totally transform them. Look out for more unusual grains such as quinoa, bulgar wheat and wild rice. For added fibre opt for wholemeal varieties of pasta or rice.

SALAD SUCCESS

Follow these simple guidelines for the perfect salad every time!

When buying salad leaves pick ones that look fresh and spritely with no wilting or browning leaves. If you buy a ready prepared bag of salad leaves, give the bag a good shake and check for any signs of deterioration. Only buy as much as you need as salad greens don't retain their freshness for long and salad bags once opened will need to be consumed within 24 hours.

Store salad leaves in a plastic box or unsealed bag in the salad drawer of the refrigerator. If you've bought unwashed greens from a farmers' market or greengrocer don't worry about rinsing them until you are ready to use them as they will stay fresher for longer.

Bunches of cut fresh herbs with long stalks such as parsley and mint should be stored in the refrigerator with their stalks in a jug of water. Other herbs with shorter stems and cut basil sprigs are best kept in an open plastic bag or loosely wrapped in damp kitchen paper and stored in the salad drawer of the refrigerator.

To prepare salad leaves, carefully separate them from the stem if necessary. Rinse in a large bowl or sink full of cold water to remove fine grit and dirt. Discard any limp, wilted or browning leaves. Shake the excess water off the leaves then spin until dry in a salad spinner or gently pat dry with a clean tea towel. The leaves should be thoroughly dry before tossing with a dressing otherwise they will dilute the dressing. Salad leaves can be washed and dried a few hours before serving but will need to be stored, without dressing, in the refrigerator.

Most dressings can also be prepared in advance and stored in the refrigerator. Remember they will need a thorough whisking or shaking before adding to the salad and it's also worth checking seasoning at this time as well.

Dress leafy salads just before serving and only use enough of the dressing to lightly coat the leaves otherwise they will quickly wilt. Pour the dressing into a large chilled serving bowl then pile the salad loosely on top. Using salad servers or clean hands, gently toss the leaves in the dressing.

If you're catering for a large number of people and serving a variety of different salads, then prepare the ones with grains, pulses or pasta first as they will keep the longest.

Side salads should complement and enhance the dishes they are served with, not overpower them, so choose carefully and only serve a small bowlful.

Timing is vital when serving warm salads. Prepare everything in advance including the dressing. Allow very hot foods such as chargrilled meats to cool slightly before completing the salad to prevent the heat wilting salad leaves too quickly.

SALAD TECHNIQUES

PEELING TOMATOES

Choose firm and ripe tomatoes for peeling. With the tip of a sharp knife, score a cross through the skin at the base of each tomato. Place in a heatproof bowl, cover with boiling water and leave for 2–3 minutes until the skins begin to wrinkle and split. Drain and plunge the tomatoes into a bowl of ice cold water for 1–2 minutes then drain again and peel the skin away with your fingertips.

BLANCHING VEGETABLES

This technique is used to lightly cook vegetables such as green beans and asparagus, yet still retain their crispness and colour. Plunge the prepared vegetables into a pan of boiling water for about 2 minutes. Quickly drain into a colander then refresh under cold running water to stop the cooking process.

VEGETABLE RIBBONS

These look impressive and are easy to make. Run a swivel-headed vegetable peeler along the length of firm vegetables such as carrot, cucumber or courgette. Use immediately or sprinkle with a little cold water and cover and chill in the refrigerator for no longer than a couple of hours before serving.

INTRODUCTION TO OILS

Edible oil has a rich history shared by many cultures over many centuries. It is used as a cooking medium, a preservative, a medicine and, best of all, food. The Chinese and Japanese developed methods to extract oil from soya plants; Mediterranean people use olives; Mexicans and North Americans are fond of peanuts and sunflower seeds; and in Africa, palms and coconuts provide the basis for oil. Other sources of oil are cotton, safflower seeds, watermelon seeds, grape seeds, rapeseed, corn, nuts, avocados and, of course, animals.

Thanks to the popularity of the Mediterranean diet, olive oil has captured the world's attention with its health-inducing benefits. Other beneficial oils, such as rapeseed, are almost flavourless and present the perfect backdrop for flavourful additions.

There are just a few guidelines to follow before getting started. The most important to remember is this: oil improperly stored can encourage the growth of bacteria. When herbs or vegetables with a high water content (like garlic) are mixed with oil and stored in a non-refrigerated place, an oxygen-free environment is created that can lead to botulism.

GARLIC, CHILLI & OREGANO OIL

5 garlic cloves
2 tbsp red hot chilli
1 tsp dried oregano
250 ml/9 fl oz rapeseed oil

Preheat the oven to 150°C/300°F/Gas Mark 2.

Cut the garlic cloves in half lengthways. Using gloves, remove the seeds from the chilli and chop the flesh into small pieces equalling 2 tablespoons.

Combine the garlic, chilli and oregano with the oil in an ovenproof glass dish. Place in the centre of the oven and heat for 1½–2 hours. The temperature of the oil should reach 120°C/250°F if you are using a digital thermometer.

Remove from the oven, leave to cool and then strain through muslin into a clean jar. Store covered in the refrigerator. You can also leave the garlic and chilli pieces in the oil and strain before using.

PARSLEY & CORIANDER OIL

10 g/$^{1}/_{4}$ oz fresh parsley leaves
10 g/$^{1}/_{4}$ oz fresh coriander leaves
250 ml/9 fl oz rapeseed oil

Wash and drain the leaves. Prepare a pot of water, bring to the boil and submerge the leaves. Blanch for 5 seconds. Drain the leaves and dry well.

Heat the oil in a saucepan, bring almost to the boil and allow to simmer for 1–2 minutes.

Combine the warmed oil and leaves in a blender bowl or food processor. Process until well combined. Pour through muslin and strain into a clean jar. Cover and refrigerate.

INTRODUCTION TO VINEGARS

Our ancestors were very wise about vinegar. The ancient Babylonians used it as a preservative, the Romans drank it, Helen of Troy bathed in it and Cleopatra dissolved a pearl in it to prove that she could consume a fortune in a single meal. It is mentioned numerous times in the Bible, and Hippocrates recommended its therapeutic properties.

As with oils, there are many types of vinegars: balsamic (produced from selected grapes and fermented for a long time), red and white wine vinegar, rice vinegar and cider vinegar. There are also speciality vinegars like raspberry, sherry and champagne vinegar.

Good vinegar can be utilized in so many ways. It is used to prepare and preserve food. It also has health-giving properties: a tablespoon a day of cider vinegar is said to be most beneficial. Even its hygienic properties are well known; your grandmother was right when she told you that there is nothing like a spray of vinegar for cleaning.

Best of all, vinegar plays an important role in dressings, sauces and mustards. It adds just the right kick to a barbecue sauce; it brings tanginess to a vinaigrette; it sweetens a wine reduction sauce. Infusing vinegar with other flavours is a great way to add yet another layer of aroma and flavour.

LEMON, BASIL & CHIVE VINEGAR

zest of ½ lemon
5 basil leaves
10 stalks chives
250 ml/9 fl oz white wine vinegar

When peeling the lemon for the zest (using only half the lemon), be sure to avoid the white pith. Wash and dry the basil leaves and the chives, then crush them or chop roughly. Place the zest, basil and chives in a clean jar.

In a saucepan over a medium heat, heat the white wine vinegar until it starts to bubble around the edges of the pan. Wait until it cools just a little, then add it to the jar with the other ingredients. When it is completely cool, cover the jar and store in a cool, dark and dry place.

ROSEMARY & GARLIC BALSAMIC VINEGAR

ten 5-cm/2-inch sprigs rosemary
4 garlic cloves
250 ml/9 fl oz balsamic vinegar

Wash the rosemary sprigs, dry and tear off the leaves from the stems. Cut the garlic cloves in half lengthways. Combine the leaves and garlic halves in a clean jar.

In a saucepan over a medium heat, heat the balsamic vinegar until it just starts to bubble around the edges of the pan. Wait until it cools a little, then pour into the jar with the rosemary and garlic. When it is completely cool, cover the jar and store in a cool, dark place. Check occasionally to see whether the vinegar has reached the desired strength.

Before using, strain the vinegar through a fine sieve or muslin into clean jars. Add a fresh sprig of rosemary for decoration and again cover and store in a cool, dark place.

MEAT

WARM BEEF SALAD NIÇOISE

Place the steaks in a shallow dish. Blend the vinegar with 1 tablespoon of orange juice and 1 teaspoon of mustard. Pour over the steaks, cover and leave in the refrigerator for at least 30 minutes. Turn over halfway through the marinating time. Place the eggs in a pan and cover with cold water. Bring to the boil, then reduce the heat to a simmer and cook for 10 minutes. Remove and plunge the eggs into cold water. Once cold, shell and reserve.

Meanwhile, place the potatoes in a saucepan and cover with cold water. Bring to the boil, cover and simmer for 15 minutes, or until tender when pierced with a fork. Drain and reserve.

Bring a saucepan of water to the boil, add the beans and cook for 5 minutes, or until just tender. Drain, plunge into cold water and drain again. Arrange the potatoes and beans on top of the salad leaves together with the yellow pepper, cherry tomatoes and olives, if using. Blend the remaining orange juice and mustard with the olive oil and reserve.

Heat a griddle pan until smoking. Drain the steaks and cook for 3–5 minutes on each side or according to personal preference. Slice the steaks and arrange on top of the salad, then pour over the dressing and serve.

SERVES 4

4 fillet steaks, about 115 g/4 oz each, trimmed of any visible fat

2 tbsp red wine vinegar

2 tbsp orange juice

2 tsp ready-made English mustard

2 eggs

175 g/6 oz new potatoes

115 g/4 oz French beans, trimmed

175 g/6 oz mixed salad leaves, such as baby spinach, rocket and mizuna

1 yellow pepper, peeled, skinned and cut into strips

175 g/6 oz cherry tomatoes, halved

black olives, stoned (optional)

2 tsp extra virgin olive oil

ROAST BEEF SALAD

Preheat the oven to 220°C/425°F/Gas Mark 7. Rub the beef with pepper to taste and Worcestershire sauce. Heat 2 tablespoons of the oil in a small roasting tin over a high heat, add the beef and sear on all sides. Transfer the dish to the preheated oven and roast for 30 minutes. Remove and leave to cool.

Bring a saucepan of water to the boil, add the beans and cook for 5 minutes, or until just tender. Remove with a slotted spoon and refresh the beans under cold running water. Drain and put into a large bowl.

Return the bean cooking water to the boil, add the pasta and cook for 11 minutes, or until tender. Drain, return to the saucepan and toss with the remaining oil.

Add the pasta to the beans with the onions, radicchio leaves, olives and hazelnuts, mix gently and transfer to a serving bowl or dish. Arrange some thinly sliced beef on top.

To make the dressing, put all the ingredients into a small screw-top jar and shake until well blended. Pour over the salad and serve immediately with extra sliced beef. Season with extra pepper, if liked.

SERVES 4

750 g/1 lb 10 oz beef fillet, trimmed of any visible fat

2 tsp Worcestershire sauce

3 tbsp olive oil

400 g/14 oz French beans

100 g/3½ oz dried orecchiette pasta

2 red onions, finely sliced

1 large head radicchio

50 g/1¾ oz green olives, stoned

50 g/1¾ oz shelled hazelnuts, whole

pepper

dressing

1 tsp Dijon mustard

2 tbsp white wine vinegar

5 tbsp olive oil

BEEF SATAY SALAD

SERVES 4

2 sirloin steaks, about 225 g/8 oz each, trimmed of any visible fat

2 tbsp soy sauce

1 tbsp lime juice

1 garlic clove, crushed

1 tsp dried chilli flakes

350 g/12 oz Chinese leaves, shredded

¼ cucumber, thinly sliced

4 spring onions, sliced

fresh coriander leaves and sliced red chilli pepper, to garnish

lime wedges, to serve

satay dressing

2 tbsp crunchy peanut butter

3 tbsp coconut milk

1 tbsp soy sauce

1 tbsp lime juice

2 tsp soft brown sugar

Place the steaks in a shallow dish. Mix together the soy sauce, lime juice, garlic and chilli flakes and pour over the steaks. Cover and leave to marinate at room temperature for 1 hour.

Heat a cast-iron griddle pan until very hot. Add the steaks and cook for 3–5 minutes on each side, depending on how well done you like your steak. Transfer the steaks to a plate and cover and leave to rest for 5 minutes.

To make the satay dressing, place all the ingredients in a small saucepan and heat gently, stirring all the time, until the peanut butter has melted. Simmer for 1 minute. If the dressing becomes too thick add a little water and stir well to make a pouring consistency.

Mix together the Chinese leaves, cucumber and spring onions and place on a serving platter. Thinly slice the steaks and arrange on top of the salad. Drizzle over the satay dressing and garnish with coriander leaves and chilli pepper. Serve with lime wedges.

SICHUAN NUMBING BEEF SALAD

Slice the beef into neat strips measuring about 1 x 4 cm/ ½ x 1½ inches. Combine the marinade ingredients and pour over the beef. Leave at room temperature for 30 minutes or in the refrigerator for up to 2 days.

Cook the noodles in a saucepan of boiling water for 4 minutes, or according to the instructions on the packet, until soft. Allow to cool. Snip into shorter lengths. Whisk the dressing ingredients until well blended. Combine the noodles, onion, radishes and salad leaves in a large bowl. Whisk the dressing again and pour two thirds of it over the salad. Toss to distribute the noodles, then divide between individual serving plates.

Heat a wok over a medium–high heat, then add the groundnut oil and the Sichuan pepper. Stir for a few seconds to flavour the oil. Add the beef and marinade, and stir-fry for 4–5 minutes until caramelized. To make the dressing, whisk the ingredients together in a bowl until well blended. Pour over the remaining dressing.

SERVES 4

350 g/12 oz sirloin steak, trimmed of any visible fat

90 g/3½ oz egg noodles

1 small red onion, halved and thinly sliced into crescents

6 radishes, sliced

4 good handfuls of peppery leaves such as tatsoi, mustard greens and rocket

1½ tbsp groundnut oil

1 tsp Sichuan pepper, crushed

marinade

4 tsp Chinese rice wine or dry sherry

½ tbsp soy sauce

4 tsp sugar

2 tbsp hoisin sauce

2.5-cm/1-inch piece fresh ginger, squeezed in a garlic press

dressing

2 tsp Sichuan pepper, crushed

1½ tbsp light soy sauce

1½ tbsp rice vinegar

2 tbsp cold-pressed sesame oil

STEAK WALDORF SALAD

Heat a cast-iron griddle pan or heavy-based frying pan over a medium heat. Brush each steak with oil and season to taste with pepper. Add the steaks to the pan and cook for 6–7 minutes for rare or 8–10 minutes for medium, turning the steaks frequently and brushing once or twice with oil. Remove from the pan and reserve.

Meanwhile, stir the mustard into the mayonnaise. Put the lemon juice into a large bowl. Peel and core the apples, then cut them into small chunks and immediately toss them in the lemon juice. Stir in the mustard mayonnaise. Add the celery and walnuts to the apple mixture and toss together.

Arrange the salad leaves on 4 plates, then divide the apple mixture between them. Very thinly slice the steaks, arrange on top of the salad and serve immediately with bread.

SERVES 4

2 fillet steaks, about 175 g/6 oz each and 2.5 cm/1 inch thick

olive oil or sunflower oil, for brushing

1 tbsp wholegrain mustard

150 ml/5 fl oz mayonnaise

1 tbsp lemon juice

500 g/1 lb 2 oz eating apples

4 celery sticks, thinly sliced

70 g/2½ oz walnut halves, broken into pieces

100 g/3½ oz mixed salad leaves

pepper

fresh wholemeal bread, to serve

WARM BACON & EGG SALAD

SERVES 4

2 cos lettuce hearts, roughly torn

4 eggs

2 tbsp sunflower oil

2 thick slices of white bread, crusts removed, cut into cubes

225 g/8 oz smoked bacon lardons

12 cherry tomatoes, halved

dressing

2 tbsp extra virgin olive oil

1 tbsp red wine vinegar

1 tsp Dijon mustard

pepper

To make the dressing, put all the ingredients into a small screw-top jar and shake until well blended. Put the lettuce leaves in a salad bowl.

Place the eggs in a saucepan and cover with cold water. Bring to the boil and boil for 4 minutes. Drain and plunge the eggs into cold water for 2 minutes. Peel off the shells and cut into quarters.

Heat the sunflower oil in a large frying pan and fry the bread cubes for 3–4 minutes, turning frequently until golden brown. Remove with a slotted spoon and set aside.

Add the bacon lardons to the pan and fry over a medium–high heat until crisp and golden. Add the tomatoes and dressing to the pan and cook for a further minute.

Gently toss the bacon, tomatoes and dressing into the salad leaves. Add the quartered eggs and scatter over the croûtons. Serve immediately.

BLT SALAD

SERVES 4

8 thick rashers back bacon

1 iceberg lettuce, cut into 12 wedges

2 beef tomatoes, sliced into wedges

¼ cucumber, thickly sliced

½ ripe avocado, sliced

1 tbsp lemon juice

85 g/3 oz Cheddar cheese, roughly grated (optional)

dressing

4 tbsp mayonnaise

2 tbsp soured cream

1 tbsp milk

2 tsp wholegrain mustard

salt and pepper

Preheat the grill to high. Place the bacon rashers on the grill pan and grill for 3–4 minutes, turning once, until crisp.

To make the dressing, place the mayonnaise, soured cream, milk and mustard in a bowl and whisk together until smooth. Season with salt and pepper.

Divide the lettuce wedges between 4 serving plates with the tomatoes and cucumber. Toss the avocado slices in the lemon juice and add to the salads.

Drizzle the dressing over the salads. Halve the bacon rashers and stack on top of the salads. Sprinkle over the grated cheese, if using. Serve immediately.

CRISPY SPINACH & BACON SALAD

Heat 2 tablespoons of the olive oil over a high heat in a large frying pan. Add the diced bacon to the pan and cook for 3–4 minutes, or until crisp. Remove with a slotted spoon, draining carefully, and set aside.

Toss the cubes of bread in the fat remaining in the pan over a high heat for about 4 minutes, or until crisp and golden. Remove the croûtons with a slotted spoon, draining carefully, and set them aside.

Add the remaining oil to the frying pan and heat. Toss the spinach in the oil over a high heat for about 3 minutes, or until it has just wilted. Turn into a serving bowl and sprinkle with the bacon and croûtons. Serve immediately.

SERVES 4

4 tbsp olive oil

4 rashers of streaky bacon, diced

1 thick slice of white bread, crusts removed, cut into cubes

450 g/1 lb fresh spinach, torn or shredded

WALNUT, PEAR & CRISPY BACON SALAD

SERVES 4

4 lean bacon rashers

85 g/3 oz walnut halves

2 Red William pears, cored and sliced lengthways

1 tbsp lemon juice

175 g/6 oz watercress, tough stalks removed

dressing

3 tbsp extra virgin olive oil

2 tbsp lemon juice

½ tsp clear honey

salt and pepper

Preheat the grill to high. Place the bacon rashers on the grill pan and grill for 3–4 minutes, turning once, until crisp. Set aside to cool, then cut into 1-cm/½-inch pieces.

Meanwhile, heat a dry frying pan over a medium heat and lightly toast the walnuts, shaking the pan frequently, for 3 minutes, or until lightly browned. Set aside to cool.

Toss the pears in the lemon juice to prevent discoloration. Put the watercress, walnuts, pears and bacon into a salad bowl.

To make the dressing, place the oil, lemon juice and honey in a bowl and whisk together until smooth. Season to taste with salt and pepper, then pour over the salad. Toss well to combine and serve.

ROAST PORK & PUMPKIN SALAD

Preheat the oven to 200°C/400°F/Gas Mark 6. Cut the pumpkin halves into wedges about 4 cm/1½ inches wide. Very lightly brush the pumpkin and onion wedges with the olive oil, place in a roasting pan and roast for 25–30 minutes until the pumpkin and onions are tender but holding their shape.

Bring a saucepan of water to the boil, add the beans and cook for 5 minutes, or until just tender. Remove with a slotted spoon and refresh the beans under cold running water. Drain and put into a large bowl.

Remove the pumpkin and onion wedges from the oven as soon as they are tender-crisp and leave to cool completely. When the pumpkin is cool, peel and cut into bite-sized pieces.

To make the dressing, put all the ingredients into a small screw-top jar and shake until well blended.

Put the pumpkins, onions, beans, pork, rocket, feta, pine kernels and parsley in a large bowl, pour over the dressing and gently toss until coated. Divide between individual bowls and serve.

SERVES 4–6

1 small pumpkin, about 1.6 kg/3½ lb, cut in half and deseeded

2 red onions, cut into wedges

olive oil, for brushing

100 g/3½ oz French beans, topped and tailed and cut in half

600 g/1 lb 5 oz roast pork, trimmed of any visible fat and cut into bite-sized chunks

large handful of rocket leaves

100 g/3½ oz feta cheese, drained and crumbled

2 tbsp toasted pine kernels

2 tbsp chopped fresh flat-leaf parsley

salt and pepper

dressing

6 tbsp extra virgin olive oil

3 tbsp balsamic vinegar

½ tsp sugar

½ tsp Dijon or wholegrain mustard

HOISIN PORK WITH RIBBON SALAD

Slice the pork fillet into 2 pieces and place in a shallow dish. Pour over the hoi sin sauce, cover and leave to marinate at room temperature for 1 hour.

Preheat the oven to 190°C/375°F/ Gas Mark 5.

Place the pork fillet on a wire rack set over a roasting tin half filled with water (this helps to keep the pork moist during cooking). Roast for 35–40 minutes until the pork is cooked through and lightly charred in places. Cool for 10 minutes.

Use a potato peeler to peel the carrots and cucumber into thin ribbons. Place in a bowl and toss together with the spring onions and radishes.

Heat a non-stick frying pan and add the sesame seeds. Cook over a medium heat for 3–4 minutes until lightly toasted. Add to the salad. To make the dressing, put the sesame oil and vinegar into a small screw-top jar and shake until well blended. Pour half over the salad and toss well to mix.

Slice the pork fillet and arrange on individual serving plates with the ribbon salad on the side. Drizzle the rest of the dressing over the pork and serve immediately.

SERVES 4

450 g/1 lb pork fillet

3 tbsp hoi sin sauce

175 g/6 oz carrots

½ cucumber

4 spring onions, finely shredded

4 radishes, very thinly sliced

2 tbsp sesame seeds

dressing

2 tbsp toasted sesame oil

2 tbsp rice vinegar

PORK & CUCUMBER SALAD

SERVES 4

450 g/1 lb pork fillet, trimmed of any visible fat

6 spring onions, halved lengthways and sliced into 3

1 ridge cucumber

4 handfuls shredded crisp lettuce

20 g/¾ oz coriander leaves

10 g/¼ oz mint leaves

4 tbsp dry-roasted peanuts, lightly crushed

finely grated zest of 1 lime

1 tsp salt

1 tsp sugar

2 tsp sesame oil

1 tbsp groundnut oil

marinade

2 small red chillies, deseeded and very finely chopped

4 tbsp sugar

3 tbsp Thai fish sauce

4 tbsp lime juice

4 tbsp rice vinegar

Thinly slice the pork diagonally. Cut each slice in half lengthways. Put in a bowl with the spring onions.

Peel the cucumber, halve lengthways and scoop out the seeds. Thinly slice diagonally and put in a bowl.

To make the marinade, use a large mortar and pestle and pound the chopped chillies and the sugar to a watery red paste. Add the fish sauce, lime juice and rice vinegar, stirring to dissolve the sugar. Pour into a measuring jug. Pour one half over the pork and onions, and one half over the cucumber. Leave to marinate for 1 hour, then drain, reserving the cucumber marinade.

Put the shredded lettuce, coriander and mint in a bowl, and toss to mix. Divide between individual serving plates. Arrange the cucumber slices on top and dress with the reserved marinade.

Mix the nuts with the lime zest, salt and sugar.

Drain the pork and discard the marinade. Heat a wok over a high heat, then add the oils. Stir-fry the pork for 5 minutes until cooked through and slightly caramelized. Arrange the pork slices on top of the cucumber and sprinkle with the nut mixture. Serve immediately.

SPINACH & PANCETTA SALAD

SERVES 4

- 275 g/9¾ oz baby spinach leaves
- 2 tbsp olive oil
- 150 g/5½ oz pancetta
- 280 g/10 oz mixed wild mushrooms, sliced

dressing

- 5 tbsp olive oil
- 1 tbsp balsamic vinegar
- 1 tsp Dijon mustard
- pinch of sugar
- salt and pepper

To make the dressing, put all the ingredients into a small screw-top jar and shake until well blended. Rinse the baby spinach under cold running water, then drain and place in a large salad bowl.

Heat the oil in a large frying pan. Add the pancetta and fry for 3 minutes. Add the mushrooms and cook for 3–4 minutes, or until tender.

Pour the dressing into the frying pan and immediately turn the fried mixture and dressing into the bowl with the spinach. Toss until coated with the dressing and serve immediately.

PASTRAMI & PEPPER ANTIPASTI SALAD

Tear the lettuce into small chunks and place in a serving bowl. Drain the pepper antipasti and sunblush tomatoes reserving 4 tbsp of the oil. Roughly chop the peppers and tomatoes and toss into the lettuce with the olives.

To make the dressing, put the reserved oil and the rest of the dressing ingredients into a small screw-top jar and shake until well blended. Pour half the dressing over the salad and toss well to mix. Arrange the pastrami in ruffles on top of the salad. Serve drizzled with the rest of the dressing and garnished with basil leaves.

SERVES 4

1 iceberg lettuce

1 x 285 g jar chargrilled pepper antipasti in oil

115 g/4 oz sunblush tomatoes

115 g/4 oz green olives, stoned

115 g/4 oz wafer thin pastrami

fresh basil leaves, to garnish

dressing

2 tbsp balsamic vinegar

1 tsp Dijon mustard

pinch of sugar

salt and pepper

ARTICHOKE & PROSCIUTTO SALAD

SERVES 4

275 g/9¾ oz canned artichoke hearts in oil, drained

4 small tomatoes

25 g/1 oz sun-dried tomatoes in oil, drained

40 g/1½ oz prosciutto

25 g/1 oz black olives, stoned and halved

handful of fresh basil sprigs

fresh crusty bread, to serve

dressing

3 tbsp olive oil

1 tbsp white wine vinegar

1 garlic clove, crushed

½ tsp mild mustard

1 tsp clear honey

salt and pepper

Make sure the artichoke hearts are thoroughly drained, then cut them into quarters and put into a serving bowl. Cut each fresh tomato into wedges. Slice the sun-dried tomatoes into thin strips. Cut the prosciutto into thin strips and add to the bowl with the tomatoes and olive halves.

Keeping a few basil sprigs whole for garnishing, tear the remainder of the leaves into small pieces and add to the bowl containing the other salad ingredients.

To make the dressing, put all the ingredients into a small screw-top jar and shake until well blended.

Pour the dressing over the salad and toss together. Garnish the salad with a few basil sprigs and serve with crusty bread.

HAM & SALAMI SALAD WITH FIGS

Trim the stems of the figs to leave just a short length, then cut the figs into quarters.

Arrange the ham and salami on a large serving platter.

Wash and dry the herbs and rocket and put in a bowl with the prepared figs.

To make the dressing, whisk all the ingredients together in a small bowl. Pour over the herbs and salad leaves and carefully turn the figs and leaves in the dressing until they are well coated.

Spoon the figs and salad onto the meat and arrange around the platter.

SERVES 6

9–12 ripe figs, depending on size

6 thin slices dry-cured Italian ham

12 thin slices salami

1 small bunch fresh basil sprigs

few fresh mint sprigs

1 small bunch rocket leaves

dressing

2 tbsp freshly squeezed lemon juice

4 tbsp extra virgin olive oil

salt and pepper

SALAMI PASTA SALAD

SERVES 4–6

350 g/12 oz dried penne pasta

2 tbsp pesto sauce

3 tbsp olive oil

1 orange pepper, deseeded and diced

1 yellow pepper, deseeded and diced

1 red onion, finely diced

85 g/3 oz black olives, stoned

115 g/4 oz cherry tomatoes, halved

175 g/6 oz piece Milano salami, cut into small chunks

125 g/4½ oz mozzarella cheese, torn into small pieces

salt and pepper

fresh basil sprigs, to garnish

Bring a large saucepan of lightly salted water to the boil. Add the pasta and return to the boil. Cook for 10–12 minutes until just tender.

Drain the pasta well and transfer to a bowl. Mix together the pesto sauce and olive oil and stir into the hot pasta. Leave to cool, stirring occasionally.

Add the peppers, onion, olives, tomatoes, salami and mozzarella cheese to the pasta and toss well to mix. Season to taste with salt and pepper. Serve garnished with the basil sprigs.

ONION & HERB SALAD WITH CHORIZO

SERVES 2

- 1 tbsp sunflower oil
- 1 small onion, finely sliced
- 250 g/9 oz canned butter beans, drained and rinsed
- 1 tsp balsamic vinegar
- 2 chorizo sausages, sliced diagonally
- 1 small tomato, diced
- 2 tbsp harissa paste
- 85 g/3 oz mixed herb salad

Heat the oil in a non-stick frying pan over a medium heat, add the onion and cook, stirring frequently, until softened but not browned. Add the beans and cook for a further 1 minute, then add the vinegar, stirring well. Keep warm.

Meanwhile, heat a separate dry frying pan over a medium heat, add the chorizo slices and cook, turning occasionally, until lightly browned. Remove with a slotted spoon and drain on kitchen paper.

Mix the tomato and harissa paste together in a small bowl. Divide the herb salad between 2 plates, spoon over the bean mixture and scatter over the warm chorizo slices. Top with a spoonful of the tomato and harissa mixture and serve immediately.

SPICY SAUSAGE PASTA SALAD

Bring a large saucepan of lightly salted water to the boil. Add the pasta and return to the boil. Cook for 10–12 minutes until just tender. Drain the pasta and reserve.

Heat the oil in a pan over a medium heat. Add the onion and fry until translucent. Stir in the garlic, yellow pepper and sliced sausage and cook for about 3–4 minutes, stirring once or twice.

Add the wine, vinegar and reserved pasta to the pan, stir to blend well and bring the mixture just to the boil over a medium heat.

Arrange the salad leaves on 4 large serving plates, spoon over the warm sausage and pasta mixture and serve immediately.

SERVES 4

125 g/4½ oz dried conchiglie pasta

2 tbsp olive oil

1 medium onion, chopped

2 garlic cloves, crushed

1 small yellow pepper, deseeded and cut into matchsticks

175 g/6 oz spicy pork sausage, such as chorizo, Italian pepperoni or salami, skinned and sliced

2 tbsp red wine

1 tbsp red wine vinegar

125 g/4½ oz mixed salad leaves

salt

HOT SAUSAGE & POTATO SALAD

Place the potatoes in a saucepan and cover with cold water. Bring to the boil, cover and simmer for 15 minutes, or until tender when pierced with a fork.

Meanwhile, heat the sunflower oil in a large frying pan and fry the sausages for 5 minutes. Add the onions to the pan and continue cooking for a further 8–10 minutes, turning frequently, until the sausages are cooked through and the onions are golden and tender. Remove the onions and sausages from the pan and drain on kitchen paper. Slice each sausage diagonally into 4 pieces.

Drain the potatoes and place in a large bowl with the onions and sausages.

To make the dressing, put all the ingredients in a small screw-top jar and shake until well blended. Pour over the hot salad and toss well to coat. Serve immediately, garnished with chopped parsley, if using.

SERVES 4

700 g/1 lb 9 oz new potatoes, halved

1 tbsp sunflower oil

6 thick pork sausages

2 onions, sliced into thin wedges

chopped fresh flat-leaf parsley, to garnish (optional)

dressing

4 tbsp olive oil

1 tbsp white wine vinegar

2 tsp wholegrain mustard

2 tsp clear honey

salt and pepper

ARTICHOKE & CHORIZO SALAD

SERVES 8

12 small globe artichokes

juice of ½ lemon

2 tbsp olive oil

1 small orange-fleshed melon, such as cantaloupe

200 g/7 oz chorizo sausage, outer casing removed

fresh tarragon or flat-leaf parsley sprigs, to garnish

dressing

3 tbsp extra virgin olive oil

1 tbsp red wine vinegar

1 tsp prepared mustard

1 tbsp chopped fresh tarragon

salt and pepper

Cut the artichokes into quarters and brush with lemon juice to prevent discoloration.

Heat the olive oil in a large, heavy-based frying pan. Add the prepared artichokes and fry, stirring frequently, for 5 minutes, or until the artichoke leaves are golden brown. Remove from the frying pan, transfer to a large serving bowl and leave to cool.

To prepare the melon, cut in half and scoop out the seeds with a spoon. Cut the flesh into bite-sized cubes. Add to the cooled artichokes. Cut the chorizo into bite-sized chunks and add to the melon and artichokes.

To make the dressing, put all the ingredients into a small screw-top jar and shake until well blended. Just before serving, pour the dressing over the prepared salad ingredients and toss together. Serve the salad garnished with tarragon.

GRILLED LAMB WITH YOGURT DRESSING

Mix the 2 tablespoons of oil, tomato purée, cumin, lemon juice, garlic, cayenne and salt and pepper to taste together in a non-metallic bowl. Add the lamb fillets and rub all over with the marinade. Cover the bowl and marinate in the fridge for at least 2 hours, but ideally overnight.

To make the dressing, whisk the lemon juice and honey together until the honey dissolves. Whisk in the yogurt until well blended. Stir in the herbs and add salt and pepper to taste. Cover and chill until required. Preheat the grill to high.

Remove the lamb from the fridge 15 minutes before you are ready to cook. Brush the grill rack with oil. Grill the lamb fillet, turning it once, for 10 minutes for medium and 12 minutes for well done. Leave the lamb to cool completely, then cover and chill until required.

Thinly slice the lamb fillets, then divide between 4 plates. Pour the dressing over the lamb slices, sprinkle with toasted sesame seeds and parsley and serve.

SERVES 4

2 tbsp sunflower oil, plus extra for grilling

1 tbsp tomato purée

½ tbsp ground cumin

1 tsp lemon juice

1 garlic clove, crushed

pinch of cayenne pepper

500 g/1 lb 2 oz lamb neck fillets, trimmed of any visible fat

oil, for brushing

salt and pepper

toasted sesame seeds and sprigs of fresh flat-leaf parsley, to garnish

dressing

2 tbsp fresh lemon juice

1 tsp clear honey

85 g/3 oz Greek yogurt

2 tbsp finely shredded fresh mint

2 tbsp chopped fresh flat-leaf parsley

1 tbsp finely snipped fresh chives

LAMB KOFTE & HERB SALAD

SERVES 4

400 g/14 oz lean minced lamb

1 small onion, finely chopped

2 tsp each ground coriander, ground cumin and paprika

1 tbsp chopped fresh coriander

2 tbsp chopped fresh mint

3 tbsp olive oil

6 tbsp natural yogurt

85 g/3 oz cucumber, grated

2 tsp mint sauce

115 g/4 oz mixed baby leaf and herb salad

1 tbsp lemon juice

salt and pepper

Place 8 wooden skewers in a shallow bowl of cold water and leave to soak for 30 minutes. Place the lamb, onion, spices and coriander and mint in a food processor with plenty of salt and pepper. Process for 1–2 minutes until finely minced. Transfer to a bowl and cover and chill in the refrigerator for 30 minutes. Preheat the grill to medium–high.

Divide the mixture into 8. Wrap the mixture around the soaked wooden skewers to form oval shapes. Brush with a little of the oil and grill for 15–20 minutes, turning frequently until cooked through.

Meanwhile, mix the yogurt, cucumber and mint sauce together in a small bowl and season with salt and pepper.

Place the salad leaves in a large bowl. Whisk together the rest of the oil with the lemon juice and season to taste. Pour the dressing over the salad leaves and toss to coat. Serve the hot koftes, on or off the skewers, with the salad and cucumber and mint yogurt.

POULTRY

LAYERED CHICKEN SALAD

SERVES 4

750 g/1 lb 10 oz new potatoes

1 red pepper, halved and deseeded

1 green pepper, halved and deseeded

2 small courgettes, sliced

1 small onion, thinly sliced

3 tomatoes, sliced

350 g/12 oz cooked chicken, sliced

snipped fresh chives, to garnish

dressing

150 ml/5 fl oz natural yogurt

3 tbsp mayonnaise

1 tbsp snipped fresh chives

salt and pepper

Place the potatoes in a saucepan and cover with cold water. Bring to the boil, cover and simmer for 15 minutes, or until tender when pierced with a fork. Preheat the grill to high. Place the pepper halves, skin side up, and grill until the skins blacken and begin to char.

Remove the peppers with tongs, place in a bowl and cover with clingfilm. Set aside until cool enough to handle, then peel off the skins and slice the flesh.

Bring a small pan of lightly salted water to the boil. Add the courgettes, bring back to the boil and simmer for 3 minutes. Drain, rinse under cold running water to prevent any further cooking and drain again. Set aside.

To make the dressing, whisk the yogurt, mayonnaise and snipped chives together in a small bowl until well blended. Season to taste with salt and pepper.

When the potatoes are tender, drain, cool and slice them. Add them to the dressing and mix gently to coat evenly. Spoon the potatoes on to 4 serving plates, dividing them equally.

Top each plate with one quarter of the pepper slices and courgettes. Layer one quarter of the onion and tomato slices, then the sliced chicken, on top of each serving. Garnish with snipped chives and serve immediately.

CORONATION CHICKEN SALAD

SERVES 4

- 1 tbsp sunflower oil
- 1 tbsp cashew nuts
- 1 tbsp whole blanched almonds
- 1 onion, chopped
- 1 tbsp mild curry paste
- 4 tbsp mayonnaise
- 4 tbsp natural yogurt
- 1 tbsp mango chutney
- 450 g/1 lb boneless cooked chicken, torn into large strips
- 140 g/5 oz watercress, spinach and rocket salad
- 1 small mango, peeled, stoned and sliced
- salt and pepper
- fresh coriander leaves, to garnish

Heat the oil in a frying pan. Add the cashew nuts and almonds and fry for 2–3 minutes until golden. Remove with a slotted spoon and drain on kitchen paper.

Add the onion to the pan and fry gently for 6–7 minutes until soft and golden. Stir in the curry paste and cook for a further minute. Transfer to a bowl and cool.

Stir the mayonnaise, yogurt and mango chutney into the onion and mix well. Add the chicken strips to the dressing. Toss well to coat. Season with salt and pepper.

Place the salad leaves in a shallow serving bowl. Add the curried chicken and mango slices to the bowl and toss gently into the salad leaves. Scatter over the fried nuts and serve garnished with the coriander leaves.

CHICKEN & CHEESE SALAD

SERVES 4

150 g/5½ oz rocket leaves

2 celery sticks, trimmed and sliced

½ cucumber, sliced

2 spring onions, trimmed and sliced

2 tbsp chopped fresh flat-leaf parsley

25 g/1 oz walnut pieces

350 g/12 oz boneless roast chicken, sliced

125 g/4½ oz Stilton cheese, cubed

handful of seedless red grapes, halved (optional)

salt and pepper

dressing

2 tbsp olive oil

1 tbsp sherry vinegar

1 tsp Dijon mustard

1 tbsp chopped mixed herbs

Wash the rocket leaves, pat dry with kitchen paper and put them into a large salad bowl. Add the celery, cucumber, spring onions, parsley and walnuts and mix together well. Transfer onto a large serving platter. Arrange the chicken slices over the salad, then scatter over the cheese. Add the red grapes, if using. Season well with salt and pepper.

To make the dressing, put all the ingredients into a small screw-top jar and shake until well blended. Drizzle the dressing over the salad and serve.

SMOKED CHICKEN SALAD

To make the dressing, put the avocado, lemon juice and vinegar in a food processor or blender and process until smooth, scraping down the side with a rubber spatula. Add the yogurt, garlic and tarragon leaves and process again. Season with salt and pepper to taste, then transfer to a bowl. Cover with clingfilm and chill for 2 hours.

To assemble the salad, divide the tomato slices between 4–6 individual plates. Toss the smoked chicken, watercress, beansprouts and parsley leaves together. Divide the salad ingredients between the plates.

Adjust the seasoning in the dressing, if necessary. Spoon the dressing over each salad and serve.

SERVES 4–6

2 large, juicy beefsteak tomatoes, sliced

600 g/1 lb 5 oz smoked chicken, skinned and cut into slices

250 g/9 oz fresh watercress, any thick stems or yellow leaves removed, then rinsed and patted dry

85 g/3 oz beansprouts, soaked for 20 minutes in cold water, then drained well and patted dry

leaves from several sprigs fresh flat-leaf parsley or coriander

dressing

1 ripe, soft avocado

2 tbsp lemon juice

1 tbsp tarragon vinegar

85 g/3 oz Greek yogurt

1 small garlic clove, crushed

1 tbsp chopped fresh tarragon leaves

salt and pepper

CHICKEN AVOCADO SALAD

To make the dressing, put all the ingredients into a small screw-top jar and shake until well blended.

Put the salad leaves into a bowl, add about one third of the dressing and lightly toss. Add the chicken, satsumas, celery, onion, chives and the remaining dressing and toss again.

Cut the avocados in half and remove the stone, then peel away the skin. Cut the flesh into thin slices, add to the other ingredients and gently toss together, making sure the avocado slices are completely coated with dressing so they don't discolor.

Arrange on individual plates, sprinkle with sunflower seeds and serve with pitta crisps on the side.

SERVES 4

125 g/4½ oz mixed salad leaves, such as beetroot greens, escarole, endive and radicchio, rinsed and dried

400 g/14 oz boneless cooked chicken, shredded

2 satsumas, separated into segments

2 celery sticks, thinly sliced

½ red onion, halved and thinly sliced

2 tbsp snipped fresh chives

2 avocados

toasted sunflower seeds, to garnish

pitta crisps, to serve

dressing

125 ml/4 fl oz extra virgin olive oil

3 tbsp Chinese rice wine vinegar

½ tsp Dijon mustard

salt and pepper

ROAST CHICKEN WITH PESTO CREAM SALAD

SERVES 4–6

600 g/1 lb 5 oz boneless cooked chicken, any skin removed and cut into bite-sized pieces

3 celery sticks, chopped

2 large skinned red peppers from a jar, well drained and sliced

salt and pepper

iceberg lettuce leaves, to serve

pesto cream

150 ml/5 fl oz crème fraîche or soured cream

about 4 tbsp bottled pesto sauce

To make the pesto cream, put the crème fraîche into a large bowl, then beat in the pesto sauce. Taste and add more pesto if you want a stronger flavour.

Add the chicken, celery and red peppers to the bowl and gently toss together. Add salt and pepper to taste and toss again. Cover and chill until required.

Remove the salad from the fridge 10 minutes before serving to return to room temperature. Give the salad ingredients a good stir, then divide between individual plates lined with lettuce leaves.

CHICKEN & PANCETTA CAESAR SALAD

To make the dressing, place all the ingredients in a food processor or hand blender and process until smooth.

Heat a large non-stick frying pan and add the pancetta slices. Cook over a high heat for about 2 minutes until crisp and frazzled. Remove with a slotted spoon and drain on kitchen paper. Add the chicken to the pan and fry over a medium–high heat for 5–6 minutes until golden and cooked through. Remove and drain with the pancetta.

Add the garlic and oil to the pan and stir in the bread cubes. Fry over a high heat, turning frequently, for 2–3 minutes until crisp and golden.

Place the lettuce and dressing in a serving bowl and toss together thoroughly. Add the pancetta and chicken and toss in gently. Scatter over the garlic croûtons and Parmesan cheese shavings and serve immediately.

SERVES 2

12 thin smoked pancetta slices

225 g/8 oz skinless, boneless chicken breasts, cubed

1 garlic clove, crushed

3 tbsp olive oil

1 small rustic or ciabatta roll, cut into chunky cubes

1 small cos lettuce, chopped into large pieces

fresh Parmesan cheese shavings, to serve

dressing

3 tbsp mayonnaise

2 tbsp soured cream

1 tbsp milk

1 garlic clove, crushed

½ tsp Dijon mustard

2 tbsp finely grated Parmesan cheese

2 anchovy fillets in oil, drained and finely chopped

pepper

WARM CHICKEN LIVER SALAD

Arrange the salad leaves on serving plates.

Heat the oil in a non-stick frying pan, add the onion and cook for 5 minutes, or until softened. Add the chicken livers, tarragon and mustard and cook for 3–5 minutes, stirring, until tender. Place on top of the salad leaves.

Add the vinegar, salt and pepper to the pan and heat, stirring all the time, until all the sediment has been lifted from the pan. Pour over the chicken livers and serve warm.

SERVES 4

225 g/8 oz mixed salad leaves

1 tbsp olive oil

1 small onion, finely chopped

450 g/1 lb frozen chicken livers, thawed

1 tsp chopped fresh tarragon

1 tsp wholegrain mustard

2 tbsp balsamic vinegar

salt and pepper

CHINESE CHICKEN SALAD

SERVES 4

3 boneless, skinless chicken breasts, weighing 450 g/1 lb in total, cut into bite-sized pieces

2 tsp soy sauce

¼ tsp freshly ground white pepper

2 tbsp groundnut oil, plus extra for deep-frying

50 g/1¾ oz thin rice noodles

½ head Chinese leaves, thinly sliced diagonally

3 spring onions, green parts included, sliced diagonally

40 g/1½ oz almonds with skin, sliced lengthways

sesame seeds, to garnish (optional)

dressing

5 tbsp olive oil

3 tbsp rice vinegar

3 tbsp soy sauce

a few drops sesame oil

salt and pepper

Sprinkle the chicken with the soy sauce and white pepper.

To make the dressing, whisk the ingredients together in a bowl until well blended.

Heat a wok over a high heat, then add the groundnut oil. Stir-fry the chicken for 4–5 minutes until brown and crisp. Drain on kitchen paper and allow to cool. Wipe out the wok.

Pour enough groundnut oil for deep-frying into the wok. Heat to 180°C/350°F or until a cube of bread browns in 30 seconds, then fry a few noodles at a time until puffed up and crisp. Drain on kitchen paper.

Arrange the Chinese leaves in a shallow serving dish. Place the noodles in a pile on top of the leaves on one side of the dish. Arrange the chicken, spring onion and almonds in the remaining space. Whisk the dressing again and pour over the salad. Dress with the sesame seeds, if using. Serve.

BANG BANG CHICKEN SALAD

SERVES 4

- 225 g/8 oz Chinese leaves, roughly torn
- 2 carrots, cut into thin sticks
- ½ cucumber, deseeded and cut into thin sticks
- 55 g/2 oz beansprouts
- 400 g/14 oz cooked boneless chicken breast, shredded
- 1 tbsp toasted sesame seeds
- 1 tbsp salted peanuts, chopped

dressing

- 4 tbsp smooth peanut butter
- 2 tbsp sweet chilli sauce
- 1 tbsp soy sauce
- 1 tbsp rice vinegar
- 1 tbsp sunflower oil
- 1 tbsp roasted peanut oil

To make the dressing, place the peanut butter in a heatproof bowl. Set the bowl over a saucepan of simmering water and stir until the peanut butter has melted. Stir in the chilli sauce, soy sauce and rice vinegar. Remove from the heat and gradually stir in the sunflower and peanut oil to make a dressing with a smooth pouring consistency.

Arrange the Chinese leaves on a serving platter and top with the carrots, cucumber and beansprouts. Top with the shredded chicken and spoon over the warm dressing. Sprinkle with the sesame seeds and peanuts and serve immediately.

GINGERED CHICKEN SALAD

Mix together the spring onions, ginger, crushed garlic and 2 tablespoons of the oil in a shallow dish and add the chicken. Cover and marinate for at least 3 hours. Lift the meat out of the marinade and set aside.

Heat a wok over a high heat, then add the remaining oil. Cook the onion for 1–2 minutes. Add the chopped garlic, baby corn, mangetout and pepper and cook for 2–3 minutes, until just tender. Add the cucumber, half the soy sauce, the sugar and the basil and mix gently.

Soak the noodles for 2–3 minutes or until tender, and drain well. Sprinkle the remaining soy sauce over them and arrange on plates. Top with the cooked vegetables.

Add a little more oil to the wok if necessary and cook the chicken over a fairly high heat until browned on all sides and cooked through. Arrange the chicken cubes on top of the salad and serve hot or warm.

SERVES 4

4 spring onions, chopped

2.5-cm/1-inch piece fresh ginger, finely chopped

4 garlic cloves, 2 crushed and 2 chopped

3 tbsp vegetable or groundnut oil

4 skinless, boneless chicken breasts, cut into cubes

1 onion, sliced

115 g/4 oz baby corn, halved

115 g/4 oz mangetout, halved lengthways

1 red pepper, deseeded and sliced

7.5-cm/3-inch piece cucumber, peeled, deseeded and sliced

4 tbsp soy sauce

1 tbsp soft light brown sugar

few Thai basil leaves

175 g/6 oz fine egg noodles

NOODLE BASKETS WITH CHICKEN SALAD

SERVES 4

groundnut or corn oil, for deep-frying

250 g/9 oz fresh fine or medium egg noodles

chicken salad

6 tbsp soured cream

6 tbsp mayonnaise

2.5-cm/1-inch piece fresh ginger, grated

grated rind and juice of 1 lime

4 skinless, boneless chicken thighs, poached and cooled, then cut into thin strips

1 carrot, grated

1 cucumber, cut in half lengthways, deseeded and sliced

1 tbsp finely chopped fresh coriander

1 tbsp finely chopped fresh mint

1 tbsp finely chopped fresh parsley

salt and pepper

To shape the noodle baskets, you will need a special set of 2 long-handled wire baskets that clip inside each other, available from specialist kitchen stores. Dip the larger wire basket in oil, then line it completely and evenly with one quarter of the noodles. Dip the smaller wire basket in oil, then position it inside the larger basket and clip it into position.

Heat the oil in a wok to 180°C/350°F, or until a cube of bread browns in 30 seconds. Lower the baskets into the oil and deep-fry for 2–3 minutes, or until the noodles are golden brown. Remove the baskets from the oil and drain on kitchen paper. Unclip the 2 wire baskets and carefully remove the small one. Use a palette knife, if necessary, to prise the noodle basket from the wire frame. Repeat to make 3 more baskets. Set aside to cool.

To make the chicken salad, combine the soured cream, mayonnaise, ginger and lime rind. Gradually add the lime juice until you get the flavour you like. Stir in the chicken, carrot and cucumber and season to taste with salt and pepper. Cover and chill.

To serve, stir in the herbs and spoon the salad into the noodle baskets.

CAJUN CHICKEN SALAD

SERVES 4

- 4 skinless, boneless chicken breasts, about 140 g/5 oz each
- 4 tsp Cajun seasoning
- 2 tsp sunflower oil (optional)
- 1 ripe mango, peeled, stoned and cut into thick slices
- 200 g/7 oz mixed salad leaves
- 1 red onion, thinly sliced and cut in half
- 175 g/6 oz cooked beetroot, diced
- 85 g/3 oz radishes, sliced
- 55 g/2 oz walnut halves
- sesame seeds, to garnish

dressing

- 4 tbsp walnut oil
- 1–2 tsp Dijon mustard
- 1 tbsp lemon juice
- salt and pepper

Make 3 diagonal slashes across each chicken breast. Put the chicken into a shallow dish and sprinkle all over with the Cajun seasoning. Cover and refrigerate for at least 30 minutes.

When ready to cook, brush a griddle pan with the sunflower oil, if using. Heat over a high heat until very hot and a few drops of water sprinkled into the pan sizzle immediately. Add the chicken and cook for 7–8 minutes on each side, or until thoroughly cooked. If still slightly pink in the centre, cook a little longer. Remove the chicken and reserve.

Add the mango slices to the pan and cook for 2 minutes on each side. Remove and reserve.

Meanwhile, arrange the salad leaves in a salad bowl and scatter over the onion, beetroot, radishes and walnut halves.

To make the dressing, put all the ingredients into a small screw-top jar and shake until well blended. Pour over the salad.

Add the mango, top with the chicken breast and sprinkle with sesame seeds. Serve.

BBQ CHICKEN SALAD

Place the oil, tomato sauce, honey, Worcestershire sauce and mustard powder in a shallow bowl and mix together well. Season with salt and pepper. Add the chicken and turn to coat in the marinade. Cover and leave to marinate in the refrigerator for 3–4 hours or overnight.

Preheat the oven to 200°C/400°F/ Gas Mark 6. Place the chicken on a rack set over a roasting tin. Spoon over any remaining marinade and roast in the oven for 40–45 minutes until cooked through and lightly charred in places. Cool for 5 minutes.

Arrange the lettuce leaves, carrots, sweetcorn and pepper on 4 serving plates. To make the dressing, mix the soured cream and chives in a small bowl and season with salt and pepper.

Thickly slice each chicken breast and arrange on the salads. Serve with fresh chives, if using.

SERVES 4

1 tbsp olive oil
4 tbsp tomato sauce
1 tbsp clear honey
1 tbsp Worcestershire sauce
1 tsp mustard powder
4 boneless chicken breasts (with skin), about 140 g/5 oz each
4 Little Gem lettuces, separated into leaves
4 carrots, roughly grated
6 tbsp canned sweetcorn, drained
½ red pepper, thinly sliced
salt and pepper
fresh chives, to garnish (optional)

dressing

6 tbsp soured cream
2 tbsp snipped fresh chives

CHICKEN FAJITA SALAD

SERVES 4

450 g/1 lb skinless, boneless chicken breasts, sliced

2 tbsp lime juice

2 tbsp olive oil

1 tsp each pepper, dried oregano and mild chilli powder

1 onion, sliced into thin wedges

1 red pepper, deseeded and thickly sliced

200 g/7 oz mixed salad leaves

lime slices and soured cream, to serve

avocado salsa

1 ripe avocado, finely diced

2 ripe tomatoes, finely chopped

1 tbsp fresh chopped coriander

1 tbsp lime juice

salt and pepper

To make the avocado salsa, place the avocado in a small bowl and stir in the tomatoes, coriander and lime juice. Season with salt and pepper. Cover the surface closely with clingfilm and chill in the refrigerator.

Place the chicken in a bowl. Add the lime juice, oil, pepper, oregano and chilli powder. Toss to coat. Cover and leave to marinate at room temperature for 1 hour.

Heat a cast iron griddle pan until very hot and add the chicken slices. Cook for 5–6 minutes, turning occasionally, until the chicken is cooked through and charred in places. Remove from the pan and keep warm. Add the onion and pepper to the pan and cook for 3–4 minutes, turning once until just tender.

Divide the salad leaves between 4 serving plates and top with the chicken, onion and pepper. Serve immediately with the avocado salsa, lime slices and soured cream.

HONEY & CHICKEN PASTA SALAD

To make the dressing, place all the ingredients in a small bowl and whisk together.

Bring a large saucepan of lightly salted water to the boil. Add the pasta and return to the boil. Cook for 10–12 minutes until just tender.

Meanwhile, heat the oil in a large frying pan. Add the onion and garlic and fry for 5 minutes. Add the chicken and cook, stirring frequently, for 3–4 minutes until just cooked through. Stir the mustard and honey into the pan and cook for a further 2–3 minutes until the chicken and onion are golden brown and sticky.

Drain the pasta and transfer to a serving bowl. Pour over the dressing and toss well. Stir in the chicken and onion and leave to cool.

Gently stir the tomatoes and mizuna into the pasta. Serve garnished with the thyme leaves.

SERVES 4

250 g/9 oz dried fusilli pasta

2 tbsp olive oil

1 onion, thinly sliced

1 garlic clove, crushed

400 g/14 oz skinless, boneless chicken breast, thinly sliced

2 tbsp wholegrain mustard

2 tbsp clear honey

175 g/6 oz cherry tomatoes, halved

handful of mizuna or rocket leaves

fresh thyme leaves, to garnish

dressing

3 tbsp olive oil

1 tbsp sherry vinegar

2 tsp clear honey

1 tbsp fresh thyme leaves

salt and pepper

BRAISED CHICKEN SALAD

Preheat the oven to 180°C/350°F/Gas Mark 4. Heat the olive oil in an ovenproof casserole over medium–high heat. Add the chicken and fry for 15 minutes, turning, until golden all over. Pour in the wine and simmer for 2 minutes, then add the onion, carrot, celery and bay leaf. Season with salt and pepper. Cover tightly and transfer to the oven. Bake for 45–50 minutes, turning every 20 minutes, until the juices from the thickest part of the thigh run clear when pierced with a skewer. Discard the liquid and solids. When cool enough to handle, remove and discard the skin. Strip the meat from the bone, slicing any large chunks into bite-sized pieces.

Arrange the chicken in a dish. Sprinkle with salt, a few peppercorns and the bay leaves. Pour in enough oil to generously coat. Cover tightly with clingfilm and marinate in the refrigerator for 1–2 days.

Remove the chicken from the fridge 2 hours before serving. Place in a colander set over a bowl to drain, and leave to stand until the oil has liquefied.

To make the salad, combine the spinach, celery and chicory in a large serving dish. Toss with salt, enough oil from the chicken to just coat the leaves, and the wine vinegar. Arrange the chicken on top, discarding the peppercorns and bay leaves. Sprinkle with the balsamic vinegar before serving.

SERVES 4

3 tbsp olive oil

1 chicken, weighing about 1.3 kg/3 lb

200 ml/7 fl oz dry white wine

1 onion, chopped

1 carrot, chopped

1 celery stalk, chopped

1 fresh bay leaf

salt and pepper

marinade

1 tsp black peppercorns

4 fresh bay leaves

125 ml/4 fl oz olive oil

salad

150 g/5½ oz baby spinach leaves, chopped

5 tender celery stalks

1 head chicory

1 tsp wine vinegar

1 tsp balsamic vinegar

CHICKEN, RAISIN & PINE KERNEL SALAD

SERVES 6–8

4 large skinless, boneless chicken breasts, about 600 g/1 lb 5 oz in total

5 tbsp olive oil

1 garlic clove, finely chopped

150 g/5½ oz pine kernels

100 ml/3½ fl oz extra virgin olive oil

1 small bunch of fresh flat-leaf parsley, finely chopped

salt and pepper

dressing

50 ml/2 fl oz red wine vinegar

25 g/1 oz caster sugar

1 bay leaf

pared rind of 1 lemon

150 g/5½ oz seedless raisins

To make the dressing, put the vinegar, sugar, bay leaf and lemon rind in a saucepan and bring to the boil, then remove from the heat. Stir in the raisins and leave to cool.

When the dressing is cool, slice the chicken breasts widthways into very thin slices. Heat the olive oil in a large frying pan, add the chicken slices and cook over a medium heat, stirring occasionally, for 8–10 minutes until lightly browned and tender.

Add the garlic and pine kernels and cook, stirring constantly and shaking the pan, for 1 minute, or until the pine kernels are golden brown. Season to taste with salt and pepper.

Pour the cooled dressing into a large bowl, discarding the bay leaf and lemon rind. Add the extra virgin olive oil and whisk together. Season to taste with salt and pepper. Add the chicken mixture and parsley and toss together. Turn the salad into a serving dish and serve warm or, if serving cold, cover and chill in the refrigerator for 2–3 hours before serving.

TURKEY COUSCOUS SALAD

Place the couscous in a large heatproof bowl. Pour over enough boiling water to cover. Stir well, cover and leave to soak for about 15 minutes until all the liquid has been absorbed. Use a fork to break up any clumps and stir in 3 tbsp of the olive oil and the vinegar. Season with plenty of salt and pepper.

Heat the rest of the oil in a large frying pan and add the turkey and harissa paste. Fry for 3 minutes, turning frequently, until the turkey is no longer pink. Add the courgettes and onion to the pan and fry for a further 10–12 minutes, stirring occasionally, until the turkey and vegetables are golden brown and tender.

Stir the turkey and vegetables into the couscous with the apricots and pine kernels. Cool for 10 minutes then stir in the chopped coriander and adjust the seasoning to taste. Serve piled into bowls garnished with coriander sprigs.

SERVES 4

225 g/ 8 oz couscous

5 tbsp olive oil

3 tbsp red wine vinegar

350 g/12 oz turkey breast fillet, cubed

1 tsp harissa paste

175 g/6 oz courgettes, diced

1 onion, chopped

115 g/4 oz no-need-to-soak dried apricots, chopped

2 tbsp toasted pine kernels

2 tbsp chopped fresh coriander

salt and pepper

fresh coriander sprigs, to garnish

TURKEY & RICE SALAD

Reserve 3 tablespoons of the chicken stock and bring the remainder to the boil in a large saucepan. Add the rice and cook for 30 minutes, or until tender. Drain and leave to cool slightly.

Meanwhile, heat 1 tablespoon of the oil in a preheated wok or frying pan. Stir-fry the turkey over a medium heat for 3–4 minutes, or until cooked through. Using a slotted spoon, transfer the turkey to a dish. Add the mangetout and mushrooms to the wok and stir-fry for 1 minute. Add the reserved stock, bring to the boil, then reduce the heat, cover and simmer for 3–4 minutes. Transfer the vegetables to the dish and leave to cool slightly.

Thoroughly mix the rice, turkey, mangetout, mushrooms, nuts, coriander and garlic chives together, then season to taste with salt and pepper. Drizzle with the remaining sunflower oil and the vinegar and garnish with fresh garlic chives. Serve warm.

SERVES 4

1 litre/1¾ pints chicken stock

175 g/6 oz mixed long-grain and wild rice

2 tbsp sunflower or corn oil

225 g/8 oz skinless, boneless turkey breast, trimmed of all visible fat and cut into thin strips

225 g/8 oz mangetout

115 g/4 oz oyster mushrooms, torn into pieces

55 g/2 oz shelled pistachio nuts, finely chopped

2 tbsp chopped fresh coriander

1 tbsp snipped fresh garlic chives

1 tbsp balsamic vinegar

salt and pepper

fresh garlic chives, to garnish

ROAST DUCK SALAD

SERVES 4

2 duck breasts

2 Little Gem lettuces, shredded

115 g/4 oz beansprouts

1 yellow pepper, deseeded and cut into thin strips

½ cucumber, deseeded and cut into matchsticks

shredded lime zest and shredded coconut, to garnish

dressing

juice of 2 limes

3 tbsp Thai fish sauce

1 tbsp soft brown sugar

2 tsp sweet chilli sauce

2.5 cm/1 inch fresh ginger, grated

3 tbsp chopped fresh mint

3 tbsp chopped fresh basil

Preheat the oven to 200°C/400°F/Gas Mark 6. Place the duck breasts on a rack set over a roasting tin and roast in the oven for 20–30 minutes, or until cooked as desired and the skin is crisp. Remove from the oven and set aside to cool.

In a large bowl, combine the lettuces, beansprouts, pepper and cucumber. Cut the cooled duck into slices and add to the salad. Mix well.

To make the dressing, whisk together the lime juice, Thai fish sauce, sugar, chilli sauce, ginger, mint and basil in a bowl. Add the dressing to the salad and toss well.

Turn the salad out onto a serving platter and garnish with the lime zest and shredded coconut before serving.

WARM DUCK, SHALLOT & ORANGE SALAD

Halve and squeeze the juice from 1 of the oranges. Using a serrated knife remove all the peel and white pith from the other orange and halve and thinly slice.

Preheat the oven to 200°C/400°F/Gas Mark 6. Season the duck fillets with salt and pepper. Heat a large heavy-based frying pan and add the duck fillets, skin side down. Cook over a medium–high heat for 5–6 minutes until the skin is golden brown. Turn over and cook for a further minute. Place the duck fillets in a shallow roasting tin and roast in the preheated oven for 10 minutes. Cook for a little longer if you prefer the duck well done.

Add the shallots to the pan and turn to coat in the duck fat. Fry gently for 7–8 minutes until golden and tender. Remove with a slotted spoon and keep warm. Pour the orange juice into the pan and bring to the boil. Whisk in the sugar, oil and vinegar and simmer for 2–3 minutes until just syrupy. Season to taste with salt and pepper.

Arrange the spinach, chard leaves and orange slices on 4 serving plates. Slice each duck fillet and place on top of the salad with the shallots. Spoon over the warm dressing and serve immediately.

SERVES 4

2 large oranges

4 duck breast fillets, about 175 g/6 oz each

12 small shallots, halved

1 tbsp sugar

2 tbsp olive oil

1 tbsp red wine vinegar

55 g/2 oz baby spinach leaves

55 g/2 oz baby red chard leaves

salt and pepper

DUCKLING & RADISH SALAD

SERVES 4

350 g/12 oz boneless duckling breasts

2 tbsp plain flour

1 egg

2 tbsp water

2 tbsp sesame seeds

3 tbsp sesame oil

½ head Chinese leaves, shredded

3 celery sticks, sliced finely

8 radishes, trimmed and halved

fresh basil leaves, to garnish

salt and pepper

dressing

finely grated rind of 1 lime

2 tbsp lime juice

2 tbsp olive oil

1 tbsp light soy sauce

1 tbsp chopped fresh basil

Put each duckling breast between sheets of greaseproof paper or clingfilm. Use a meat mallet or rolling pin to beat them out and flatten them slightly.

Sprinkle the flour onto a large plate and season with salt and pepper. Beat the egg and water together in a shallow bowl, then sprinkle the sesame seeds on to a separate plate.

Dip the duckling breasts first into the seasoned flour, then into the egg mixture and finally into the sesame seeds, to coat the duckling evenly. Heat the sesame oil in a preheated wok or large frying pan.

Fry the duckling breasts over a medium heat for about 8 minutes, turning once. To test whether they are cooked, insert a sharp knife into the thickest part – the juices should run clear. Lift them out and drain on kitchen paper.

To make the dressing for the salad, whisk together the lime rind and juice, olive oil, soy sauce and chopped basil. Season with a little salt and pepper.

Arrange the Chinese leaves, celery and radishes on a serving plate. Slice the duckling breasts thinly and place on top of the salad.

Drizzle with the dressing and garnish with fresh basil leaves. Serve immediately.

DUCK SALAD WITH SWEET CHILLI DRESSING

SERVES 4

2 duck leg portions, about 175 g/6 oz each

300 ml/½ pt boiling water

1 tsp Chinese five-spice powder

175 g/6 oz mangetout

1 small iceberg lettuce, finely shredded

2 celery sticks, very thinly sliced

6 spring onions, finely shredded

dressing

1 tbsp sunflower oil

3 tbsp sweet chilli sauce

1 tbsp rice vinegar

salt and pepper

Preheat the oven to 200°C/400°F/Gas Mark 6. Place the duck legs in a roasting tin and pour the boiling water over the skin. Drain off the water and pat the skins dry with kitchen paper.

Rub the Chinese five-spice powder into the duck skin. Roast the duck legs in the preheated oven for 1¼ – 1½ hours until cooked through with golden crispy skin. Cool for 10 minutes.

To make the dressing, place all the ingredients in a small bowl and whisk together.

Bring a small saucepan of water to the boil and add the mangetout. Cook for 2 minutes then drain and refresh under cold running water. Thinly slice the mangetout lengthways and place in a bowl with the lettuce, celery and nearly all the spring onions. Toss well to mix.

Peel off the crispy skin from the roast duck and cut into thin strips. Using 2 forks pull and shred all the duck flesh from the bones.

Arrange the salad on a platter and top with the shredded duck and crispy skin. Drizzle over the dressing and garnish with the rest of the spring onions. Serve immediately.

DUCK & NOODLE SALAD WITH PEANUT SAUCE

Preheat the grill to high. Cut the carrots, celery and cucumber into thin strips and set aside.

Grill the duck breasts for about 5 minutes on each side until cooked through. Leave to cool.

Meanwhile, heat all the ingredients for the peanut sauce in a small saucepan until combined and the sugar has dissolved completely. Stir until smooth.

Slice the duck breasts. Divide the noodles among 3 serving bowls. Place the reserved carrots, celery and cucumber on top of the noodles, arrange the duck slices on top and drizzle with the sauce. Serve immediately.

SERVES 3

2 carrots, peeled

2 celery sticks

1 cucumber

three 140-g/5-oz duck breasts

350 g/12 oz rice noodles, cooked according to the instructions on the packet, rinsed and drained

peanut sauce

2 garlic cloves, crushed

2 tbsp dark brown sugar

2 tbsp peanut butter

2 tbsp coconut cream

2 tbsp soy sauce

2 tbsp rice vinegar

2 tbsp sesame oil

½ tsp pepper

½ tsp Chinese five-spice powder

½ tsp ground ginger

FISH & SEAFOOD

SALAD NIÇOISE

SERVES 4

- 2 fresh tuna steaks, about 2 cm/ 3/4 inch thick
- olive oil, for brushing
- 250 g/9 oz French beans, topped and tailed
- 125 ml/4 fl oz vinaigrette or garlic vinaigrette dressing
- 2 hearts of lettuce, leaves separated
- 3 large hard-boiled eggs, quartered
- 2 juicy vine-ripened tomatoes, cut into wedges
- 50 g/1 3/4 oz anchovy fillets in oil, drained
- 55 g/2 oz Niçoise olives, stoned
- salt and pepper

Heat a ridged cast-iron griddle pan over a high heat until you can feel the heat rising from the surface. Brush the tuna steaks with oil, place oiled side down on the hot pan, and chargrill for 2 minutes. Lightly brush the top side of the tuna steaks with more oil. Use a pair of tongs to turn the tuna steaks over, then season to taste with salt and pepper. Continue chargrilling for a further 2 minutes for rare or up to 4 minutes for well done. Leave to cool.

Meanwhile, bring a saucepan of salted water to the boil. Add the beans to the pan and return to the boil, then boil for 3 minutes, or until tender-crisp. Drain the beans and immediately transfer them to a large bowl. Pour over the vinaigrette and stir together, then leave the beans to cool in the dressing.

Bring a saucepan of water to the boil, add the beans and cook for 5 minutes, or until just tender. Remove with a slotted spoon and refresh the beans under cold running water. Drain and put into a large bowl. Arrange the hard-boiled eggs and tomatoes around the side. Place the anchovy fillets over the salad, then scatter with the olives. Pour over the vinaigrette and stir together.

CARAMELIZED TUNA SALAD

To make the dressing, heat a small wok over high heat. Add the oil and fry the ginger and chilli for a few seconds. Add the soy sauce, Thai fish sauce and tamarind paste. Stir for 30 seconds, then add the sugar and stir until dissolved. Remove the wok from the heat and set aside.

Rinse the beansprouts in boiling water and drain. Blot dry with kitchen paper. Peel the cucumber, halve lengthways and scoop out the seeds. Thinly slice the flesh diagonally.

Put the beansprouts, cucumber, coriander and mint leaves in a bowl. Season with a pinch of salt and a few drops of toasted sesame oil. Toss to combine, then divide between individual serving plates.

Heat a wok over a high heat, then add the groundnut and sesame oils. Quickly stir-fry the tuna, turning with tongs, until coloured on the outside but still slightly red in the middle. Arrange the tuna chunks on top of the salad.

Reheat the dressing, thinning with a spoonful of water if necessary, and pour over the tuna. Sprinkle with the crushed peanuts and serve immediately.

SERVES 4

175 g/6 oz beansprouts

10-cm/4-inch piece of cucumber

20 g/¾ oz coriander leaves

20 g/¾ oz mint leaves

1 tsp sesame oil, plus a few drops for drizzling

1 tbsp groundnut oil

450 g/1 lb fresh tuna, cut into 2.5-cm/1-inch chunks

salt

salted roasted peanuts, crushed, to garnish

dressing

2 tsp rapeseed oil

1 tsp finely chopped fresh ginger

½–1 small red chilli, deseeded and finely chopped

4 tbsp light soy sauce

1 tbsp Thai fish sauce

1 tbsp tamarind paste

6 tbsp soft brown sugar

TUNA, LENTIL & POTATO SALAD

SERVES 4

- 200 g/7 oz Puy or brown lentils
- 2 tbsp olive oil, plus extra for brushing
- 300 g/10½ oz baby new potatoes
- 1 Little Gem lettuce
- 4 fresh tuna steaks, about 100 g/3½ oz each
- 12 small cherry tomatoes, halved
- 40 g/1½ oz rocket leaves
- salt and pepper

dressing

- 5 tbsp fruity olive oil
- 1 tbsp balsamic vinegar
- 2 tsp red wine vinegar
- 1 tsp smooth Dijon mustard
- 1 tsp soft light brown sugar

Cook the lentils in a saucepan of boiling water for 25 minutes, or until tender. Drain, tip into a bowl and stir in the oil.

Meanwhile, place the potatoes in a saucepan and cover with cold water. Bring to the boil, cover and simmer for 15 minutes, or until tender when pierced with a fork.

Break off the outer lettuce leaves and cut the heart into 8 evenly sized pieces. Arrange on 4 individual serving plates.

To make the dressing, put all the ingredients into a small screw-top jar and shake until well blended.

When the potatoes are nearly cooked, lightly brush a ridged griddle pan with oil and heat over a high heat. When very hot, add the tuna steaks and cook for 1½ minutes on each side to sear. Remove to a chopping board and cut each steak into 6 chunks.

Drain the potatoes and roughly chop any larger ones. Arrange with the lentils, tuna and tomatoes on the serving plates, sprinkle over the rocket leaves and spoon over the dressing. Serve immediately.

TUNA & TWO-BEAN SALAD

SERVES 4

200 g/7 oz French beans

400 g/14 oz canned small white beans, such as haricot, rinsed and drained

4 spring onions, finely chopped

2 fresh tuna steaks, about 225 g/8 oz each and 2 cm/¾ inch thick

olive oil, for brushing

250 g/9 oz cherry tomatoes, halved

handful lettuce leaves

salt and pepper

fresh mint and flat-leaf parsley sprigs, to garnish

dressing

handful of fresh mint leaves, shredded

handful of fresh flat-leaf parsley leaves, chopped

1 garlic clove, crushed

4 tbsp extra virgin olive oil

1 tbsp red wine vinegar

salt and pepper

To make the dressing, put all the ingredients into a small screw-top jar and shake until well blended.

Bring a saucepan of lightly salted water to the boil. Add the French beans and cook for 3 minutes. Add the white beans and cook for a further 4 minutes until the French beans are tender-crisp and the white beans are heated through. Drain well and add to the bowl with the dressing and spring onions. Toss together.

To cook the tuna, heat a ridged griddle pan over a high heat. Lightly brush the tuna steaks with oil, then season to taste with salt and pepper. Cook the steaks for 2 minutes, then turn over and cook on the other side for a further 2 minutes for rare or up to 4 minutes for well done.

Remove the tuna from the griddle pan and leave to rest for 2 minutes, or alternatively leave until completely cool. When ready to serve, add the tomatoes to the bean mixture and toss lightly. Line a serving platter with lettuce leaves and pile on the bean salad. Place the tuna over the top. Serve warm or at room temperature, garnished with the herbs.

TUNA & HERBED PASTA SALAD

SERVES 4

200 g/7 oz dried fusilli pasta

1 red pepper, deseeded and cut into quarters

150 g/5½ oz asparagus spears

1 red onion, sliced

4 tomatoes, sliced

200 g/7 oz canned tuna in brine, drained and flaked

dressing

6 tbsp basil-flavoured oil or extra virgin olive oil

3 tbsp white wine vinegar

1 tbsp lime juice

1 tsp mustard

1 tsp honey

4 tbsp chopped fresh basil, plus extra sprigs to garnish

Bring a large saucepan of lightly salted water to the boil. Add the pasta and return to the boil. Cook for 10–12 minutes until just tender. Meanwhile, preheat the grill to high.

Put the pepper quarters under the grill and cook for 10–12 minutes until the skins begin to blacken. Transfer to a plastic bag, seal and set aside.

Bring a separate pan of water to the boil, add the asparagus, and blanch for 4 minutes.

Drain and plunge into cold water, then drain again. Remove the pasta from the heat, drain, and set aside to cool. Remove the pepper quarters from the bag and peel off the skins.

Slice the pepper into strips. To make the dressing, put all the dressing ingredients in a large bowl and stir together well. Add the pasta, pepper strips, asparagus, onion, tomatoes and tuna.

Toss together gently, then divide among serving bowls. Garnish with basil sprigs and serve.

TOMATO, SALMON & PRAWN SALAD

SERVES 4

- 115 g/4 oz cherry or baby plum tomatoes
- handful lettuce leaves
- 4 ripe tomatoes, roughly chopped
- 100 g/3½ oz smoked salmon
- 200 g/7 oz large cooked prawns, thawed if frozen
- pepper

dressing

- 1 tbsp Dijon mustard
- 2 tsp caster sugar
- 2 tsp red wine vinegar
- 2 tbsp medium olive oil
- few fresh dill sprigs, plus extra to garnish

Halve most of the cherry tomatoes. Place the lettuce leaves around the edge of a bowl and add all the tomatoes and cherry tomatoes. Using scissors, snip the smoked salmon into strips and scatter over the tomatoes, then add the prawns.

To make the dressing, mix the mustard, sugar, vinegar and oil together in a small bowl, then tear most of the dill sprigs into it. Mix well and pour over the salad. Toss well to coat the salad with the dressing. Snip the remaining dill over the top and season to taste with pepper.

SMOKED SALMON & ROCKET SALAD

Shred the rocket and arrange in 4 individual bowls. Scatter over the chopped parsley and spring onions.

Halve, peel and stone the avocados and cut into thin slices or small chunks. Brush with the lemon juice to prevent discoloration, then divide between the salad bowls. Mix together gently. Cut the smoked salmon into strips and scatter over the top.

To make the dressing, put the mayonnaise in a bowl, then add the lime juice, lime rind and chopped parsley. Mix together well. Spoon some of the dressing on top of each salad and garnish with parsley sprigs.

SERVES 4

50 g/1¾ oz rocket leaves

1 tbsp chopped fresh flat-leaf parsley

2 spring onions, finely diced

2 large avocados

1 tbsp lemon juice

250 g/9 oz smoked salmon

dressing

150 ml/5 fl oz mayonnaise

2 tbsp lime juice

finely grated rind of 1 lime

1 tbsp chopped fresh flat-leaf parsley, plus extra sprigs to garnish

TERIYAKI SALMON SALAD

SERVES 4

- 6 spring onions, finely shredded
- 4 salmon fillets (with skin), about 115 g/4 oz each
- 4 tbsp teriyaki sauce
- 225 g/8 oz thread egg noodles
- 2 tsp toasted sesame oil
- 1 tsp grated fresh ginger
- 1 green pepper, finely shredded
- 2 carrots, finely shredded
- 2 tbsp sesame seeds
- 2 tbsp rice vinegar
- salt and pepper
- lime wedges, to serve

Place half the shredded spring onions in a small bowl of cold water with a couple of ice cubes. Leave in the refrigerator for at least 1 hour until the spring onions are curly.

Put the salmon fillets in a shallow dish and pour over the teriyaki sauce. Cover and leave to marinate at room temperature for 30 minutes.

Cook the noodles in a saucepan of boiling water for 4 minutes, or according to the instructions on the packet, until soft. Drain well and refresh under cold running water. Transfer to a bowl.

Heat the oil in a wok and add the ginger, pepper, carrot and remaining spring onions. Stir-fry for 1 minute. Add the sesame seeds and stir-fry for a further minute. Cool for 10 minutes then add to the noodles with the vinegar and toss well to mix. Season with salt and pepper.

Heat a non-stick frying pan and add the salmon fillets, skin side down. Cook for 1 minute on each side until browned. Pour in the teriyaki marinade. Reduce the heat and cook for a further 3–4 minutes on each side until just cooked through.

Divide the noodle salad between 4 serving plates and top each with a salmon fillet. Drain the spring onion curls and pat dry on kitchen paper. Arrange on top of the salmon fillets and serve with lime wedges.

WARM SALMON & MANGO SALAD

SERVES 4

- 115 g/4 oz yellow or red cherry tomatoes
- 85 g/3 oz salmon fillets, skinned and cut into small cubes
- 1 large ripe mango (about 150 g/ 5½ oz peeled fruit), peeled and cut into small chunks
- 2 tbsp orange juice
- 1 tbsp soy sauce
- 115 g/4 oz mixed salad leaves
- ½ cucumber, trimmed and sliced into batons
- 6 spring onions, trimmed and chopped

dressing

- 4 tbsp low fat natural yogurt
- 1 tsp soy sauce
- 1 tbsp finely grated orange rind

Cut half the tomatoes in half and set aside.

Thread the salmon with the whole tomatoes and half the mango chunks onto 4 kebab sticks. Mix the orange juice and soy sauce together in a small bowl and brush over the kebabs. Leave to marinate for 15 minutes, brushing with the remaining orange juice mixture at least once more.

Arrange the salad leaves on a serving platter with the reserved halved tomatoes, mango chunks, the cucumber batons and the spring onions.

Preheat the grill to high and line the grill rack with foil. To make the dressing, mix the yogurt, soy sauce and grated orange rind together in a small bowl and reserve.

Place the salmon kebabs on the grill rack, brush again with the marinade and grill for 5–7 minutes, or until the salmon is cooked. Turn the kebabs over halfway through cooking and brush with any remaining marinade.

Divide the prepared salad between 4 plates, top each with a kebab, and then drizzle with the dressing.

SMOKED TROUT, CHICORY & PEAR SALAD

Toss the sliced pears in the lemon juice to prevent discoloration. Place in a serving dish with the chicory leaves and watercress.

Flake the smoked trout, removing any skin and fine bones. Scatter over the salad with the grapes.

To make the dressing, place the crème fraîche, milk, horseradish and lemon juice in a small bowl and whisk until smooth. Season to taste with salt and pepper. Drizzle the dressing over the salad just before serving. Season with a little more pepper.

SERVES 4

2 ripe red William pears, cored and sliced

1 tbsp lemon juice

3 heads chicory, trimmed and leaves separated

55 g/2 oz watercress, tough stalks removed

225 g/8 oz smoked trout fillets

85 g/3 oz seedless green grapes, halved

dressing

4 tbsp crème fraîche

1 tbsp milk

1 tsp creamed horseradish

2 tsp lemon juice

salt and pepper

CAESAR SALAD

Bring a small, heavy-based saucepan of water to the boil.

Meanwhile, make the garlic croûtons. Heat the olive oil in a heavy-based frying pan. Add the garlic and diced bread and cook, stirring and tossing frequently, for 4–5 minutes, or until the bread is crispy and golden all over. Remove from the frying pan with a slotted spoon and drain on kitchen paper.

While the bread is frying, add the egg to the boiling water and cook for 1 minute, then remove from the saucepan and reserve.

Arrange the lettuce leaves in a salad bowl. Mix the olive oil and lemon juice together, then season to taste with salt and pepper. Crack the egg into the dressing and whisk to blend. Pour the dressing over the lettuce leaves, toss well, then add the croûtons and chopped anchovies and toss the salad again. Sprinkle with Parmesan cheese shavings and serve.

SERVES 4

4 tbsp olive oil

2 garlic cloves

5 slices white bread, crusts removed, cut into 1-cm/½-inch cubes

1 egg

2 cos lettuces or 3 Little Gem lettuces

6 tbsp olive oil

2 tbsp lemon juice

8 canned anchovy fillets, drained and roughly chopped

salt and pepper

fresh Parmesan cheese shavings, to serve

ANCHOVY & OLIVE SALAD

SERVES 4

125 g /4½ oz mixed lettuce leaves

12 cherry tomatoes, halved

20 black olives, stoned and halved

6 canned anchovy fillets, drained and thinly sliced

1 tbsp chopped fresh oregano

lemon wedges, to garnish

fresh crusty bread rolls, to serve

dressing

4 tbsp extra virgin olive oil

1 tbsp white wine vinegar

1 tbsp lemon juice

1 tbsp chopped fresh flat-leaf parsley

salt and pepper

To make the dressing, put all the ingredients into a small bowl and stir together well.

To assemble the salad, arrange the lettuce leaves in a serving dish. Scatter the cherry tomatoes on top, followed by the olives, anchovies and oregano. Drizzle the dressing over the top.

Transfer to individual plates, garnish with lemon wedges and serve with crusty bread rolls.

WARM MACKEREL & POTATO SALAD

Make 3–4 diagonal slashes in the skin of each mackerel fillet. Mix together the coarsely ground pepper, lemon rind and juice and oil and pour over the fillets. Cover and leave to marinate at room temperature for 20 minutes. Preheat the grill to high.

Cook the mackerel fillets under the grill for 7–8 minutes, turning once, until just cooked through. Meanwhile, place the potatoes in a saucepan and cover with cold water. Bring to the boil, cover and simmer for 12–15 minutes, or until tender when pierced with a fork.

To make the dressing, whisk the olive oil, vinegar, mustard and sugar together in a bowl until well blended. Stir in the dill and season to taste with salt and pepper.

Drain the potatoes and mix gently with the spring onions and half the dressing. Arrange on 4 serving plates and scatter over the rocket leaves. Top each salad with a hot mackerel fillet and drizzle over the rest of the dressing. Garnish with fresh dill sprigs and serve.

SERVES 4

4 mackerel fillets, about 140 g/5 oz each

1 tsp coarsely ground black pepper

1 small lemon, finely pared rind and juice

1 tbsp virgin olive oil

450 g/1 lb new potatoes, sliced

4 spring onions, thinly sliced

25 g/1 oz rocket leaves

fresh dill sprigs, to garnish

dressing

5 tbsp virgin olive oil

2 tbsp white wine vinegar

1 tsp Dijon mustard

pinch of sugar

1 tbsp chopped fresh dill

salt and pepper

SEARED SWORDFISH WITH SALSA

To make the tomato and olive salsa, whisk the olive oil and vinegar together in a bowl large enough to hold all the ingredients. Gently stir in the tomatoes, olives, shallot and capers with salt and pepper to taste. Cover and chill until required.

Season the swordfish steaks on both sides with salt. Melt the butter with the oil in a frying pan large enough to hold the swordfish steaks in a single layer. (If you don't have a large enough pan, cook the steaks in 2 batches.)

Add the swordfish steaks to the pan in a single layer and fry for 5 minutes, or until golden brown, then carefully turn the fish over and continue frying about 3 minutes longer until the fish is cooked through and flakes easily. Remove the fish from the pan and set aside to cool completely. Cover and chill for at least 2 hours.

When ready to serve, remove the fish from the fridge at least 15 minutes in advance. Stir the basil into the salsa, then adjust the seasoning if necessary. Break the swordfish into large flakes and gently stir into the salsa – take care not to break up the fish too much. Arrange the fish salad in 4 bowls, spooning over any of the leftover juices and serve with slices of crusty bread.

SERVES 4

4 boneless swordfish steaks, about 140 g/5 oz each

knob of butter

1 tbsp olive oil

fresh crusty bread, to serve

tomato & olive salsa

4 tbsp extra virgin olive oil

1 tbsp red wine vinegar

600 g/1 lb 5 oz ripe, juicy beef tomatoes, cored, deseeded and finely chopped

140 g/5 oz large black olives, stoned and cut in half

1 shallot, finely chopped or thinly sliced

1 tbsp capers in brine, rinsed and dried

3 tbsp finely shredded fresh basil leaves

salt and pepper

SWEET & SOUR FISH SALAD

SERVES 4

225 g/8 oz trout fillets

225 g/8 oz white fish fillets (such as haddock or cod)

300 ml/½ pint water

1 stalk lemon grass

2 lime leaves

1 large red chilli

1 bunch spring onions, trimmed and shredded

115 g/4 oz fresh pineapple flesh, diced

1 small red pepper, deseeded and diced

1 bunch watercress, washed and trimmed

fresh snipped chives, to garnish

dressing

1 tbsp sunflower oil

1 tbsp rice wine vinegar

pinch of chilli powder

1 tsp clear honey

salt and pepper

Rinse the fish, place in a frying pan and pour over the water. Bend the lemon grass in half to bruise it and add to the pan with the lime leaves. Prick the chilli with a fork and add to the pan. Bring to the boil and simmer for 7–8 minutes. Let cool.

Drain the fish fillet thoroughly, flake the flesh away from the skin and place in a bowl. Gently stir in the spring onions, pineapple and pepper.

Arrange the washed watercress on 4 serving plates and spoon the cooked fish mixture on top.

To make the dressing, put all the ingredients into a small bowl and mix well. Spoon over the fish and serve garnished with chives.

SPICED FISH SKEWERS & TOMATO SALAD

SERVES 4

- 450 g/1 lb cod loin or monkfish, cut into 2.5-cm/1-inch cubes
- 3 tbsp lime juice
- 4 tbsp sunflower oil
- 2 tsp mild chilli powder
- 1 tsp dried oregano
- 1 lemon, cut into 8 wedges
- 225 g/8 oz cherry tomatoes, halved
- 225 g/8 oz yellow cherry tomatoes, halved
- ½ small onion, thinly sliced
- 2 tbsp roughly chopped fresh coriander
- ½ tsp sugar
- 1 tsp mild mustard
- salt and pepper

Place the fish cubes in a shallow bowl. Mix together 2 tablespoons of the lime juice and 2 tablespoons of the oil with the chilli powder and oregano. Season with salt and pepper and pour over the fish. Cover and leave to marinate at room temperature for 1 hour.

Preheat the grill to medium. Thread the fish and lemon wedges onto 8 metal skewers and cook the fish skewers for 8–10 minutes, turning occasionally, until just cooked.

Meanwhile, mix together the tomatoes, onion and coriander in a bowl. Whisk the remaining lime juice and oil together with the sugar and mustard. Pour the dressing over the tomatoes and toss well to mix. Season with salt and pepper.

Divide the tomato salad between 4 serving dishes and top each with two fish skewers. Serve immediately.

PRAWN & WHITE BEAN SALAD

Place the beans, onion, celery, prawns and garlic in a large shallow bowl. Add the lemon juice, 2 tablespoons of the oil and the chopped parsley. Season lightly with salt and pepper. Stir well then cover and set aside.

Brush the slices of bread with some of the remaining olive oil. Cook on a hot griddle for 2–3 minutes on each side until golden or toast under a hot grill. Place on 4 serving plates.

Gently stir the tomatoes and parsley leaves into the salad. Pile the salad onto the hot toasts. Drizzle over the rest of the olive oil, season with a little more pepper and serve.

SERVES 4

400 g/14 oz can haricot beans, drained and rinsed

½ red onion, finely chopped

1 celery stick, finely diced

300 g/10½ oz cooked, large peeled prawns with tails intact

1 garlic clove, finely chopped

juice of 1 lemon

5 tbsp extra virgin olive oil

2 tbsp chopped fresh flat-leaf parsley

4 thick slices country bread (pain de champagne)

85 g/3 oz baby plum tomatoes, halved

handful of fresh flat-leaf parsley leaves

salt and pepper

COCONUT & PRAWN SALAD

SERVES 4

- 200 g/7 oz brown basmati rice
- ½ tsp coriander seeds
- 2 egg whites, lightly beaten
- 100 g/3½ oz unsweetened desiccated coconut
- 24 raw tiger prawns, peeled
- ½ cucumber
- 4 spring onions, thinly sliced lengthways
- 1 tsp sesame oil
- 1 tbsp finely chopped fresh coriander

Bring a large saucepan of water to the boil, add the rice and cook for 25 minutes, or until tender. Drain and keep in a colander covered with a clean tea towel to absorb the steam.

Meanwhile, soak 8 wooden skewers in cold water for 30 minutes, then drain. Crush the coriander seeds in a mortar with a pestle. Heat a non-stick frying pan over a medium heat, add the crushed coriander seeds and cook, turning, until they begin to colour. Tip onto a plate and set aside.

Put the egg whites into a shallow bowl and the coconut into a separate bowl. Roll each prawn first in the egg whites, then in the coconut. Thread onto a skewer. Repeat so that each skewer is threaded with 3 coated prawns.

Preheat the grill to high. Using a potato peeler, peel long strips from the cucumber to create ribbons, put into a colander to drain, then toss with the spring onions and oil in a bowl and set aside.

Cook the prawns under the preheated grill for 3–4 minutes on each side, or until slightly browned.

Meanwhile, mix the rice with the toasted coriander seeds and fresh coriander and divide this and the cucumber salad between bowls. Serve with the hot prawn skewers.

LAYERED CRAYFISH SALAD

To make the dressing, put all the ingredients into a small bowl and mix well.

Divide the grated carrot, lettuce, corn and cucumber between four bowls.

Spoon over the dressing and pile the crayfish tails on top. Sprinkle with the cayenne pepper. Garnish with lemon wedges, if using. Serve.

SERVES 4

115 g/4 oz carrots, peeled and grated

1 Little Gem lettuce, shredded

85 g/3 oz canned sweetcorn kernels, drained

¼ cucumber, diced

175 g/6 oz cooked crayfish tails in brine, thoroughly drained

½ tsp cayenne pepper

lemon wedges, to garnish (optional)

dressing

8 tbsp mayonnaise

1 tbsp tomato ketchup

dash of Worcestershire sauce

1 tbsp lemon juice

salt and pepper

THAI CRAB PATTY SALAD

SERVES 4

- 2 x 170 g/5¾ oz cans white crabmeat, drained
- 140 g/ 5 oz cooked peeled prawns
- 1 tsp lime juice
- 2 tsp Thai red curry paste
- 1 tbsp beaten egg white
- 1 tbsp chopped fresh coriander
- flour, for dusting
- sunflower oil, for shallow frying
- ½ cucumber, peeled, deseeded and thinly sliced
- 225 g/8 oz beansprouts
- 25 g/1 oz salad cress
- 2 tbsp chopped fresh coriander stalks
- 1 tbsp rice vinegar
- 4 tbsp sweet chilli sauce
- salt and pepper
- fresh coriander leaves and lime wedges, to garnish

Place the crab, prawns, lime juice and curry paste in a food processor and process for a few seconds until finely minced. Add the egg white and chopped coriander and season well with salt and pepper. Process for a further few seconds until well mixed.

Transfer the mixture to a bowl and using lightly floured hands, shape into 12 small cakes. Coat lightly in the flour. Cover and chill in the refrigerator for 1 hour.

Heat the oil in a large frying pan and fry the crab cakes, in 2 batches, for 3–4 minutes until golden brown, turning once. Drain on kitchen paper.

Place the cucumber, beansprouts, salad cress and coriander stalks in a bowl and toss together with the rice vinegar. Divide between 4 serving plates. Top with the hot crabcakes and spoon over the chilli sauce. Serve garnished with coriander leaves and lime wedges.

LOBSTER & SUMMER HERB SALAD

SERVES 4–6

750–800 g/1 lb 10 oz–1 lb 12 oz freshly cooked lobster meat, cut into bite-sized chunks

1 large avocado, peeled, stoned and cut into chunky dice

4 ripe but firm tomatoes

250 g/9 oz mixed herb salad leaves

1–2 tbsp fruity olive oil

squeeze of lemon juice

salt and pepper

saffron mayonnaise

pinch of saffron threads

1 egg

1 tsp Dijon mustard

1 tbsp white wine vinegar

pinch of salt

300 ml/10 fl oz sunflower oil

To make the saffron mayonnaise, soak the saffron threads in a little warm water. Meanwhile, put the egg, mustard, vinegar and salt in a blender and whiz to combine. With the motor running, slowly trickle in about one third of the sunflower oil. Once the mixture starts to thicken, add the remaining oil more quickly. When all the oil has been incorporated, add the saffron and its soaking water and whiz to combine. Add more salt, and pepper, to taste, cover and refrigerate until required.

Put the lobster meat and avocado in a bowl. Quarter the tomatoes and remove the seeds. Cut the flesh into fairly chunky dice and add to the bowl. Season the lobster mixture to taste with salt and pepper and gently stir in enough of the mayonnaise to give everything a light coating.

Toss the salad leaves with the olive oil and lemon juice. Divide between four to six plates and top with the lobster mixture. Serve immediately.

SEAFOOD SALAD

Clean the mussels by scrubbing or scraping the shells and pulling out any beards that are attached to them. Discard any with broken shells or any that refuse to close when tapped. Put the mussels in a colander and rinse well under cold running water. Put them in a large saucepan with a little water and cook, covered, over a high heat, shaking the saucepan occasionally, for 3–4 minutes, or until the mussels have opened. Discard any mussels that remain closed. Strain the mussels, reserving the cooking liquid. Refresh the mussels under cold running water, drain and set aside.

Return the reserved cooking liquid to the saucepan and bring to the boil, add the scallops and squid and cook for 3 minutes. Remove from the heat and drain. Refresh under cold running water and drain again. Remove the mussels from their shells. Put them in a bowl with the scallops and squid and leave to cool. Cover with clingfilm and chill in the refrigerator for 45 minutes.

Divide the seafood between 4 serving plates and top with the onion. To make the dressing, combine the ingredients together in a bowl until well blended. Garnish with chopped parsley and serve with lemon wedges.

SERVES 4

250 g/9 oz live mussels

350 g/12 oz live scallops, shucked and cleaned

250 g/9 oz prepared squid, cut into rings and tentacles

1 red onion, halved and finely sliced

chopped fresh flat-leaf parsley, to garnish

lemon wedges, to serve

dressing

4 tbsp extra virgin olive oil

2 tbsp white wine vinegar

1 tbsp lemon juice

1 garlic clove, finely chopped

1 tbsp chopped fresh flat-leaf parsley

salt and pepper

SEAFOOD & SPINACH SALAD

Put the mussels into a large pan with a little water, bring to the boil and cook over a high heat for 4 minutes. Drain and reserve the liquid. Discard any mussels that remain closed. Return the reserved liquid to the pan and bring to the boil. Add the prawns and scallops and cook for 3 minutes. Drain. Remove the mussels from their shells. Rinse the mussels, prawns and scallops in cold water, drain and put them in a large bowl. Cool, cover with clingfilm and chill for 45 minutes.

Meanwhile, rinse the baby spinach leaves and transfer them to a pan with the water. Cook over a high heat for 1 minute, transfer to a colander, refresh under cold running water and drain.

To make the dressing, put all the ingredients into a small bowl and mix well. Arrange the spinach on serving dishes, then scatter over half of the spring onions. Top with the mussels, prawns and scallops, then scatter over the remaining spring onions. Drizzle over the dressing and serve.

SERVES 4

500 g/1 lb 2 oz live mussels, soaked and cleaned

100 g/3½ oz prawns, peeled and deveined

350 g/12 oz scallops

500 g/1 lb 2 oz baby spinach leaves

4 tbsp water

3 spring onions, trimmed and diced

dressing

4 tbsp extra virgin olive oil

2 tbsp white wine vinegar

1 tbsp lemon juice

1 tsp finely grated lemon rind

1 garlic clove, chopped

1 tbsp grated fresh ginger

1 small red chilli, deseeded and diced

1 tbsp chopped fresh coriander

salt and pepper

NEAPOLITAN SEAFOOD SALAD

SERVES 4

- 450 g/1 lb prepared squid, cut into strips
- 750 g/1 lb 10 oz cooked mussels
- 450 g/1 lb cooked cockles in brine
- 150 ml/5 fl oz white wine
- 300 ml/10 fl oz olive oil
- 225 g/8 oz dried campanelle pasta
- juice of 1 lemon
- 1 bunch chives, snipped
- 1 bunch fresh flat-leaf parsley, finely chopped
- 125 g/4½ oz mixed salad leaves
- salt and pepper
- 4 large tomatoes, to garnish

Put all of the seafood into a large bowl, pour over the wine and half of the olive oil, and set aside for 6 hours.

Put the seafood mixture into a saucepan and simmer over a low heat for 10 minutes. Set aside to cool.

Bring a large saucepan of lightly salted water to the boil. Add the pasta and 1 tablespoon of the remaining olive oil and cook for 10–12 minutes until just tender. Drain and refresh in cold water.

Strain off about half of the cooking liquid from the seafood and discard the rest. Mix in the lemon juice, chives, parsley and the remaining olive oil. Season to taste with salt and pepper. Drain the pasta and add to the seafood.

Shred the leaves and arrange them at the base of a salad bowl. Cut the tomatoes into quarters. Spoon the seafood salad into the bowl, garnish with the tomatoes and serve.

VEGETARIAN

TRADITIONAL GREEK SALAD

To make the dressing, put all the ingredients into a small screw-top jar and shake until well blended. Set aside. Cut the feta cheese into cubes about 2.5 cm/1 inch square. Put the lettuce, tomatoes and cucumber in a salad bowl. Scatter over the cheese and toss together.

Just before serving, whisk the dressing, pour over the salad leaves and toss together. Scatter over the olives and chopped herbs and serve.

SERVES 4

200 g/7 oz Greek feta cheese

½ head of iceberg lettuce or 1 lettuce such as cos or escarole, shredded or sliced

4 tomatoes, quartered

½ cucumber, sliced

12 Greek black olives, stoned

2 tbsp chopped fresh herbs such as oregano, flat-leaf parsley, mint or basil

dressing

6 tbsp extra virgin olive oil

2 tbsp fresh lemon juice

1 garlic clove, crushed

pinch of sugar

salt and pepper

ROASTED VEGETABLE SALAD

Preheat the oven to 200°C/400°F/Gas Mark 6. Cut all the vegetables into even-sized wedges, put into a roasting tin and scatter over the garlic.

Pour over 2 tablespoons of the olive oil and turn the vegetables in the oil until well coated. Add a little salt and pepper. Roast in the preheated oven for 40 minutes, or until tender, adding the extra olive oil if becoming too dry.

To make the dressing, put all the ingredients into a small screw-top jar and shake until well blended.

Once the vegetables are cooked, remove from the oven, arrange on a serving dish and pour over the dressing. Garnish with the basil and serve with Parmesan cheese and crusty bread.

SERVES 4

1 onion

1 aubergine, about 225 g/8 oz

1 red pepper, deseeded

1 orange pepper, deseeded

1 large courgette, about 175 g/6 oz

2–4 garlic cloves

2–4 tbsp olive oil

salt and pepper

fresh basil leaves, to garnish

fresh Parmesan shavings and fresh crusty bread, to serve

dressing

1 tbsp balsamic vinegar

2 tbsp extra virgin olive oil

TUSCAN BREAD SALAD

SERVES 4

1 small stale ciabatta loaf

2–3 tbsp cold water

6 large ripe plum tomatoes

$\frac{1}{4}$ cucumber, peeled and roughly chopped

1 small red onion, very thinly sliced

handful fresh basil leaves

dressing

4 tbsp extra virgin olive oil, plus extra to drizzle

1 tbsp red wine vinegar

pinch of sugar

2 tsp capers, drained and rinsed

salt and pepper

Tear the bread into bite-sized chunks and place in a large shallow dish. Sprinkle with the water. Roughly chop 3 of the tomatoes and add to the dish with the cucumber and onion. Stir to mix. Tear half the basil leaves and scatter over the top.

Halve the remaining tomatoes and squeeze each half to extract as much of the juice and seeds as possible into a small bowl. Discard any remaining skin and flesh.

To make the dressing, add the olive oil, vinegar, sugar and capers to the tomato juice and seeds and whisk together. Season with salt and pepper. Pour the tomato dressing over the bread slices and toss until coated. Chill in the refrigerator for at least 30 minutes. Serve garnished with the remaining basil leaves and drizzled with a little more olive oil.

TOMATO & MOZZARELLA SALAD

Using a sharp knife, cut the tomatoes into thick wedges and place in a large serving dish. Drain the mozzarella and roughly tear into pieces. Cut the avocados in half and remove the stones. Cut the flesh into slices, then arrange the mozzarella cheese and avocado with the tomatoes.

To make the dressing, mix the oil, vinegar and mustard together in a small bowl, add salt and pepper to taste, then drizzle over the salad.

Scatter the basil and olives over the top and serve immediately with fresh crusty bread.

SERVES 4

- 2 ripe beef tomatoes
- 150 g/5½ oz fresh mozzarella
- 2 avocados
- few fresh basil leaves, torn into pieces
- 20 black olives
- fresh crusty bread, to serve

dressing

- 4 tbsp olive oil
- 1½ tbsp white wine vinegar
- 1 tsp coarse-grain mustard
- salt and pepper

SUN-DRIED TOMATO SALAD

SERVES 4

- 100 g/3½ oz mixed salad leaves, such as oakleaf lettuce, baby spinach and rocket
- 500 g/1 lb 2 oz smoked mozzarella, sliced

dressing

- 140 g/5 oz sun-dried tomatoes in olive oil (drained weight), reserving the oil from the bottle
- 15 g/½ oz fresh basil, roughly shredded
- 15 g/½ oz fresh flat-leaf parsley, roughly chopped
- 1 tbsp capers, rinsed
- 1 tbsp balsamic vinegar
- 1 garlic clove, roughly chopped
- extra olive oil, if necessary
- pepper

To make the dressing, put the sun-dried tomatoes, basil, parsley, capers, vinegar and garlic in a food processor or blender. Measure the oil from the sun-dried tomatoes jar and make it up to 150 ml/5 fl oz with more olive oil if necessary. Add it to the food processor or blender and process until smooth. Season with pepper.

Divide the salad leaves between 4 individual serving plates. Top with the slices of mozzarella and spoon the dressing over them. Serve immediately.

ASPARAGUS & TOMATO SALAD

SERVES 4

225 g/8 oz asparagus spears

1 lamb's lettuce, washed and torn

25 g/1 oz rocket or mizuna leaves

450 g/1 lb ripe tomatoes, sliced

12 black olives, stoned and chopped

1 tbsp toasted pine kernels

dressing

1 tsp lemon oil

1 tbsp olive oil

1 tsp wholegrain mustard

2 tbsp balsamic vinegar

salt and pepper

Steam the asparagus spears for about 8 minutes or until tender. Rinse under cold running water to prevent them cooking any further, then cut into 5-cm/2-inch pieces.

Arrange the lettuce and rocket leaves around a salad platter to form the base of the salad. Place the sliced tomatoes in a circle on top and the asparagus in the centre. Add the olives and the pine kernels.

To make the dressing, put all the ingredients into a small screw-top jar and shake until well blended. Drizzle over the salad and serve.

CAULIFLOWER, BROCCOLI & CASHEW NUT SALAD

Heat the oil in a preheated wok, add the onions and stir-fry over a medium–high heat for 3–4 minutes, until starting to brown. Add the cauliflower and broccoli and stir-fry for 1–2 minutes. Stir in the curry paste and stir-fry for 30 seconds, then add the coconut milk, soy sauce, palm sugar and salt. Bring gently to the boil, stirring occasionally, then reduce the heat and simmer gently for 3–4 minutes, until the vegetables are almost tender.

Meanwhile, heat a separate dry frying pan until hot, add the cashew nuts and cook, shaking the pan frequently, for 2–3 minutes, until lightly browned. Add to the stir-fry with the coriander, stir well and serve immediately, garnished with the torn coriander sprigs.

SERVES 4

- 2 tbsp groundnut or vegetable oil
- 2 red onions, cut into wedges
- 1 small head cauliflower, cut into florets
- 1 small head broccoli, cut into florets
- 2 tbsp ready-made yellow curry paste or red curry paste
- 400 ml/14 fl oz canned coconut milk
- 1 tsp soy sauce
- 1 tsp palm sugar
- 1 tsp salt
- 85 g/3 oz unsalted cashew nuts
- handful of fresh coriander, chopped, plus extra sprigs, torn, to garnish

NEW POTATO & RADISH SALAD

Place the potatoes in a saucepan and cover with cold water. Bring to the boil, cover and simmer for 15 minutes, or until tender when pierced with a fork. Drain well and leave to cool. Transfer to a serving bowl and stir in the radishes.

To make the dressing, place the soured cream and milk in a bowl and whisk until smooth. Stir in the gherkins and dill and season with salt and pepper.

Pour the dressing over the potatoes and radishes and toss to coat. Add the red onion and rocket leaves and mix gently. Serve.

SERVES 4

500 g/1 lb 2 oz new potatoes, halved

8 radishes, thinly sliced

1 small red onion, thinly sliced

25 g/1 oz rocket leaves

dressing

150 ml carton soured cream

2 tbsp milk

3 gherkins, drained and finely chopped

2 tbsp chopped fresh dill

salt and pepper

WARM NEW POTATO & LENTIL SALAD

SERVES 4

85 g/3 oz puy lentils

450 g/1 lb new potatoes

6 spring onions

1 tbsp olive oil

2 tbsp balsamic vinegar

salt and pepper

Bring a large pan of water to the boil. Rinse the lentils then cook for about 20 minutes or until tender. Drain, rinse and leave to one side.

Meanwhile, place the potatoes in a saucepan and cover with cold water. Bring to the boil, cover and simmer for 15 minutes, or until tender when pierced with a fork. Drain and halve.

Trim the base from the spring onions and cut in long strips.

Put the lentils, potatoes and spring onions into a serving dish and toss with the olive oil and vinegar. Season with plenty of pepper and a little salt if required.

SWEET POTATO SALAD

Bring a saucepan of water to the boil over a medium heat. Add the sweet potato and cook for 10 minutes, or until tender. Drain, transfer to a bowl and reserve until required.

Cook the carrots in a separate saucepan of boiling water for 1 minute. Drain thoroughly and add to the sweet potato. Cut the tops off the tomatoes and scoop out the seeds. Chop the flesh and add to the bowl with the celery and beans. Mix well.

Line a large serving bowl with the mixed salad leaves. Spoon the sweet potato and bean mixture on top, then sprinkle with the sultanas and spring onions.

To make the dressing, put all the ingredients into a small screw-top jar and shake until well blended. Pour over the salad and serve.

SERVES 4

1 sweet potato, peeled and diced

4 baby carrots, halved

4 tomatoes

4 celery sticks, chopped

225 g/8 oz canned borlotti beans, drained and rinsed

115 g/4 oz mixed salad leaves, such as curly endive, rocket, radicchio and oakleaf lettuce

1 tbsp sultanas

4 spring onions, sliced diagonally

dressing

2 tbsp lemon juice

1 garlic clove, crushed

150 ml/5 fl oz natural yogurt

2 tbsp olive oil

salt and pepper

SWEET POTATO & BEAN SALAD

Peel and dice the sweet potato. Bring a saucepan of water to the boil over a medium heat. Add the sweet potato and cook for 10 minutes, or until tender. Drain, transfer to a bowl and reserve until required.

Cook the carrots in a separate pan of boiling water for 1 minute. Drain thoroughly and add to the sweet potato. Cut the tops off the tomatoes and scoop out the seeds. Chop the flesh and add to the bowl with the celery and beans. Mix well.

Line a large serving bowl with the mixed salad leaves. Spoon the sweet potato and bean mixture on top, then sprinkle with the sultanas and spring onions.

To make the dressing, place all the ingredients in a screw-top jar and shake vigorously until they are well blended. Pour over the salad and serve.

SERVES 4

1 sweet potato, peeled and diced

4 baby carrots, halved

4 tomatoes

4 celery stalks, chopped

225 g/8 oz canned cranberry beans, drained and rinsed

125 g/4½ oz mixed salad leaves, such as curly endive, rocket, radicchio, and oak leaf lettuce

1 tbsp sultanas

4 spring onions, sliced diagonally

dressing

2 tbsp lemon juice

1 garlic clove, crushed

150 ml/5 fl oz natural yogurt

2 tbsp olive oil

salt and pepper

BEAN SALAD WITH FETA

SERVES 4

- 350 g/12 oz French beans, trimmed
- 1 red onion, chopped
- 3–4 tbsp chopped fresh coriander
- 2 radishes, thinly sliced
- 75 g/2¾ oz feta cheese, crumbled
- 1 tsp chopped fresh oregano or ½ tsp dried oregano
- 2 tbsp red wine or fruit vinegar
- 5 tbsp extra virgin olive oil
- 3 ripe tomatoes, cut into wedges
- pepper

Place the beans in a saucepan and cover with cold water. Bring to the boil, cover and simmer for 15 minutes, or until tender when pierced with a fork. Drain and halve.

Transfer the beans to a bowl and add the onion, coriander, radishes and cheese.

Sprinkle the oregano over the salad, then grind pepper over to taste. Whisk the vinegar and olive oil together and pour over the salad. Toss gently to mix well.

Transfer to a serving platter, add the tomato wedges and serve at once or chill until ready to serve.

BEAN & WALNUT SALAD

Bring a large saucepan of water to the boil, add the beans and cook for 5 minutes, or until just tender. Remove with a slotted spoon and refresh the beans under cold running water. Drain and put into a mixing bowl and add the onion, garlic and cheese.

To make the dressing, put all the ingredients in a small screw-top jar and shake until well blended. Cover with clingfilm and chill for at least 30 minutes. Remove the salad from the refrigerator 10 minutes before serving. Give it a quick stir and transfer to serving dishes.

Toast the nuts in a dry frying pan over a medium heat for 2 minutes, or until they begin to brown. Sprinkle the toasted nuts over the salad and serve.

SERVES 2

450 g/1 lb French beans

1 small onion, finely chopped

1 garlic clove, chopped

4 tbsp freshly grated Parmesan cheese

2 tbsp chopped walnuts or almonds, to garnish

dressing

2 tbsp white wine vinegar

6 tbsp olive oil

2 tsp chopped fresh tarragon

salt and pepper

HERBED MIXED BEAN SALAD

SERVES 4–6

- 115 g/4 oz French beans, topped and tailed and cut into bite-sized pieces
- 115 g/4 oz shelled broad beans, grey outer skins removed if not young
- 115 g/4 oz fresh or frozen shelled peas
- 400 g/14 oz canned haricot beans, drained and rinsed
- 1 small red onion, thinly sliced
- 2 tbsp chopped fresh parsley
- 1 tbsp snipped fresh chives
- 85 g/3 oz rocket or watercress leaves
- salt and pepper

dressing

- 5 tbsp extra virgin olive oil
- 2 tbsp tarragon vinegar
- ½ tsp mixed grain mustard
- pinch of sugar

fried halloumi cheese

- olive oil, to drizzle
- 350 g/12 oz halloumi cheese, drained, patted dry and cut into 12 slices

To make the dressing, put all the ingredients into a small screw-top jar and shake until well blended. Set aside.

Prepare a bowl of iced water. Bring a saucepan of lightly salted water to the boil. Add the French beans and the broad beans and blanch for 3 minutes, or until just tender. Use a slotted spoon to remove the beans from the water and immediately transfer them to the iced water.

Return the water to the boil and blanch the peas for 3 minutes, or until tender. Remove from the water and add to the iced water to cool.

Drain the beans and peas and pat dry with kitchen paper. Transfer to a large bowl, add the dressing, haricot beans, onion and herbs and toss. Cover and chill.

To make the fried halloumi cheese, just before you are ready to serve, heat a thin layer of oil in a large frying pan over a medium–high heat. Lightly dust each slice of cheese with flour, shaking off the excess. Place as many pieces as will fit in the pan and fry for 30–60 seconds until golden brown. Flip the cheese over and continue frying until lightly browned on the other side, then remove from the pan and keep warm while you fry the remaining pieces.

Toss the salad again, add the rocket and then add extra seasoning, if necessary. Divide the salad between individual plates and arrange the hot cheese alongside. Drizzle the cheese with olive oil, grind over some pepper and serve.

PASTA SALAD WITH PEPPERS

SERVES 4

1 red pepper

1 orange pepper

280 g/10 oz dried conchiglie pasta

5 tbsp extra virgin olive oil

2 tbsp lemon juice

2 tbsp bottled pesto sauce

1 garlic clove, finely chopped

3 tbsp shredded fresh basil leaves

salt and pepper

Preheat the grill to high. Put the whole peppers on a baking sheet and place under the hot grill, turning frequently, for 15 minutes, or until charred all over. Remove with tongs and place in a bowl. Cover with crumpled kitchen paper and reserve.

Bring a large saucepan of lightly salted water to the boil. Add the pasta and return to the boil. Cook for 10–12 minutes until just tender.

Combine the olive oil, lemon juice, pesto sauce and garlic in a bowl, whisking well to mix. Drain the pasta, add it to the pesto mixture while still hot and toss well. Reserve until required.

When the peppers are cool enough to handle, peel off the skins, then cut open and remove the seeds. Chop the flesh roughly and add to the pasta with the basil. Season to taste with salt and pepper and toss well. Serve.

MARINATED PEPPER SALAD

Preheat the oven to 190°C/375°F/Gas Mark 5. Halve the peppers, keeping the stalks on. Remove the white seeds and pith. Place the peppers, cut side up, in a shallow roasting tin. Scatter over the onion and garlic, season with salt and pepper and drizzle over half the olive oil. Roast for 40 minutes until the peppers are tender. Leave to cool.

Arrange the cold peppers on a serving plate and pour over any juices left in the roasting tin. Scatter over the olives, mozzarella pearls and basil.

Whisk together the remaining olive oil with the balsamic vinegar and pour over the peppers. Cover and leave to marinate in the refrigerator for at least 2 hours (or overnight) before serving.

SERVES 4

2 red peppers

2 yellow peppers

1 red onion, roughly chopped

2 garlic cloves, chopped

6 tbsp olive oil

115 g/4 oz marinated black olives, drained

100 g/3½ oz mini mozzarella pearls, drained

2 tbsp roughly torn fresh basil leaves

2 tbsp balsamic vinegar

salt and pepper

WILD RICE SALAD

Put the wild rice and water into a large pan and bring to the boil. Stir, cover and simmer for about 40 minutes or until the rice is al dente (firm to the bite). Uncover the rice for the last few minutes of cooking to allow any excess water to evaporate.

To make the dressing, put all the ingredients into a small screw-top jar and shake until well blended. Add extra vinegar, oil or seasoning as required.

Drain the rice and turn into a large bowl. Pour over the dressing and mix in. Then mix in the chopped peppers, cucumber, orange, tomatoes, red onion and parsley. Serve.

SERVES 4

225 g/8 oz wild rice

850 ml/1½ pints water

1 each red, yellow and orange peppers, skinned, deseeded and thinly sliced

½ cucumber, halved lengthways and sliced

1 orange, peeled, pith removed and cubed

3 ripe tomatoes, cut into chunks

1 red onion, finely chopped

generous handful of chopped flat-leaf parsley

dressing

1 clove garlic, crushed

1 tbsp balsamic vinegar

2 tbsp extra virgin olive oil

salt and pepper

SPICED ORANGE & CARROT SALAD

SERVES 4

- 500 g/1lb 2 oz carrots, roughly grated
- 4 spring onions, finely shredded
- 2 oranges
- 55 g/2 oz raisins
- 3 tbsp chopped fresh coriander
- fresh coriander sprigs, to garnish (optional)

dressing

- 3 tbsp olive oil
- 3 tbsp orange juice
- 2 tsp lemon juice
- ½ tsp ground cumin
- ½ tsp ground coriander
- salt and pepper

Place the carrot and spring onions in a large bowl and toss gently to mix. Using a serrated knife remove all the peel and pith from the oranges then cut into segments between the membranes. Gently toss the orange segments into the bowl with the raisins and chopped coriander.

To make the dressing, place the olive oil, orange and lemon juice, ground cumin and coriander in a bowl and whisk together. Season to taste with salt and pepper.

Pour the dressing over the carrot salad and toss thoroughly. Cover with clingfilm and chill in the refrigerator for 30 minutes. Adjust the seasoning to taste. Serve garnished with coriander sprigs, if using.

WARM RED LENTIL SALAD

SERVES 4

- 2 tbsp olive oil
- 2 tsp cumin seeds
- 2 garlic cloves, crushed
- 2 tsp fresh ginger, grated
- 300 g/10½ oz split red lentils
- 700 ml/1¼ pints vegetable stock
- 2 tbsp chopped fresh mint
- 2 tbsp chopped fresh coriander
- 2 red onions, thinly sliced
- 200 g/7 oz baby spinach leaves
- 1 tsp hazelnut oil
- 150 g/5½ oz soft goat's cheese
- 4 tbsp Greek yogurt
- pepper

Heat half the olive oil in a large saucepan over a medium heat, add the cumin seeds, garlic and ginger and cook for 2 minutes, stirring constantly.

Stir in the lentils, then add the stock, a ladleful at a time, until it is all absorbed, stirring constantly – this will take about 20 minutes. Remove from the heat and stir in the herbs.

Meanwhile, heat the remaining olive oil in a frying pan over a medium heat, add the onions and cook, stirring frequently, for 10 minutes, or until soft and lightly browned.

Toss the spinach in the hazelnut oil in a bowl, then divide between 4 serving plates.

Mash the goat's cheese with the yogurt in a small bowl and season to taste with pepper.

Divide the lentils between the serving plates and top with the onions and goat's cheese mixture.

GOAT'S CHEESE CROÛTON & SPINACH SALAD

To make the dressing, put all the ingredients into a small screw-top jar and shake until well blended.

Preheat the grill to medium. Lightly brush the slices of French bread with olive oil. Toast the rounds for 1–2 minutes on each side until just golden. Top each with a slice of goat's cheese, season with pepper and grill for a further 1–2 minutes until the cheese has melted.

Meanwhile, place the spinach in a large bowl. Add nearly all the dressing and toss gently to coat the leaves. Divide between 2 serving plates. Add the sun blush tomatoes and top with the cheese croûtons. Drizzle over the rest of the dressing and serve immediately.

SERVES 2

6 thin slices French bread

1 tbsp olive oil

115 g/4 oz round goat's cheese (with rind)

85 g/3 oz baby spinach leaves

55 g/2 oz sun blush tomatoes, drained

dressing

3 tbsp extra virgin olive oil

1 tbsp sherry vinegar

1 tsp wholegrain mustard

pinch of sugar

salt and pepper

CHILLI-SPICED PANEER SALAD

SERVES 2

6 tbsp sunflower oil

225 g/8 oz paneer, cubed

1 tsp mustard seeds

1 tsp ground cumin

1 garlic clove, crushed

1 small green chilli pepper, deseeded and finely chopped

4 spring onions, finely chopped

85 g/3 oz baby salad leaves

tomato chutney

2 ripe tomatoes, skinned, deseeded and diced

1 shallot, finely chopped

2 tbsp sunflower oil

2 tsp lemon juice

1 tbsp chopped fresh coriander

salt and pepper

To make the tomato chutney, place all the ingredients in a small bowl and mix together well. Chill in the refrigerator for 30 minutes.

Heat the oil in a large frying pan. Add the paneer cubes and fry over a medium–high heat for 4–5 minutes, turning frequently, until golden brown all over (take care as the oil may spit). Remove the paneer with a slotted spoon and drain on kitchen paper.

Carefully pour off half the hot oil from the pan. Add the mustard seeds and ground cumin to the remaining oil and fry for a few seconds. Stir in the garlic, chilli pepper and spring onions and fry for 1–2 minutes. Return the paneer to the pan and toss to coat well in the spicy mixture.

Divide the salad leaves between 2 serving plates. Top with the hot paneer. Spoon over the tomato chutney and serve immediately.

BUCKWHEAT NOODLE SALAD

SERVES 2

200 g/7 oz buckwheat noodles

250 g/9 oz firm smoked tofu (drained weight)

200 g/7 oz white cabbage, finely shredded

250 g/9 oz carrots, finely shredded

3 spring onions, diagonally sliced

1 fresh red chilli, deseeded and finely sliced into rounds

2 tbsp sesame seeds, lightly toasted

dressing

1 tsp fresh ginger, grated

1 garlic clove, crushed

175 g/6 oz silken tofu (drained weight)

4 tsp tamari (wheat-free soy sauce)

2 tbsp sesame oil

4 tbsp hot water

salt

Cook the noodles in a saucepan of boiling water for 4 minutes, or according to the instructions on the packet, until soft.

To make the dressing, blend the ginger, garlic, silken tofu, tamari, oil and water together in a small bowl until smooth and creamy. Season to taste with salt.

Place the smoked tofu in a steamer. Steam for 5 minutes, then cut into thin slices.

Meanwhile, put the cabbage, carrots, spring onions and chilli into a bowl and toss to mix. To serve, arrange the noodles on serving plates and top with the carrot salad and slices of tofu. Spoon over the dressing and sprinkle with sesame seeds.

RED CABBAGE & BEETROOT SLAW

Place the cabbage, beetroot and apple slices in a large bowl. Add the lemon juice and mix well.

To make the dressing, place the mayonnaise, yogurt and red wine vinegar in a bowl and mix together until smooth. Pour over the salad and stir well. Season with salt and pepper and cover and chill in the refrigerator for at least 1 hour.

Stir the salad thoroughly and adjust the seasoning to taste. Sprinkle with the sunflower and pumpkin seeds just before serving.

SERVES 4

- 350 g/12 oz red cabbage, finely shredded
- 175 g/6 oz cooked beetroot, sliced into thin matchsticks
- 1 apple, cored and thinly sliced
- 1 tbsp lemon juice
- 1 tbsp sunflower seeds
- 1 tbsp pumpkin seeds
- salt and pepper

dressing

- 3 tbsp mayonnaise
- 2 tbsp Greek yogurt
- 1 tbsp red wine vinegar

HEALTH-BOOSTING

GREEK FETA SALAD

To make the dressing, put all the ingredients into a small screw-top jar and shake until well blended.

Arrange the vine leaves on a serving dish and then the tomatoes, cucumber and onion. Scatter the cheese and olives on top. Pour the dressing over the salad, season and serve.

SERVES 4

handful vine leaves

4 tomatoes, sliced

½ cucumber, peeled and sliced

1 small red onion, sliced thinly

115 g/4 oz feta cheese, cubed

8 black olives

dressing

3 tbsp extra virgin olive oil

1 tbsp lemon juice

½ tsp dried oregano

salt and pepper

SALAD WITH GARLIC DRESSING

Gently mix the cucumber batons, spring onions, tomato wedges, yellow pepper strips, celery, radishes and rocket in a large serving bowl.

To make the dressing, stir the lemon juice, garlic, natural yogurt and olive oil together in a small bowl until thoroughly combined. Season with salt and pepper to taste.

Spoon the dressing over the salad and toss to mix. Sprinkle the salad with chopped mint, if using. Serve.

SERVES 4

85 g/3 oz cucumber, cut into batons

6 spring onions, halved

2 tomatoes, deseeded and cut into 8 wedges

1 yellow pepper, deseeded and cut into strips

2 celery sticks, cut into strips

4 radishes, quartered

85 g/3 oz rocket

chopped fresh mint, to garnish (optional)

dressing

2 tbsp lemon juice

1 garlic clove, crushed

150 ml/5 fl oz natural yogurt

2 tbsp olive oil

salt and pepper

NUTTY BEETROOT SALAD

SERVES 4

- 3 tbsp red wine vinegar or fruit vinegar
- 3 cooked beetroot, grated
- 2 tart apples, such as Granny Smith
- 2 tbsp lemon juice
- 4 large handfuls mixed salad leaves, to serve
- 4 tbsp pecans, to garnish

dressing

- 50 ml/2 fl oz plain yogurt
- 50 ml/2 fl oz mayonnaise
- 1 garlic clove, chopped
- 1 tbsp chopped fresh dill
- salt and pepper

Sprinkle vinegar over the beetroot, cover with clingfilm and chill for at least 4 hours.

Core and slice the apples, place the slices in a dish and sprinkle with the lemon juice to prevent discoloration.

Combine the dressing ingredients in a small bowl. Remove the beetroot from the refrigerator and dress. Add the apples to the beetroot and mix gently to coat with the salad dressing.

To serve, arrange a handful of salad leaves on each plate and top with a large spoonful of the apple and beetroot mixture.

Toast the pecans in a dry frying pan over a medium heat for 2 minutes, or until they begin to brown. Sprinkle over the beetroot and apple to garnish.

BULGAR WHEAT SALAD

Preheat the oven to 200°C/400°F/Gas Mark 6. Place the halved tomatoes in a roasting tin, cut side up. Scatter over the garlic, sugar and sea salt and drizzle with 2 tablespoons of the olive oil. Roast in the preheated oven for 20 minutes until soft. Cool.

Place the bulgar wheat in a heatproof bowl and pour over enough boiling water to cover the grains. Cover the bowl and leave for 30 minutes until all the liquid has been absorbed. Pour over the vinegar and the rest of the olive oil and stir thoroughly with a fork. Season well with salt and pepper.

Stir the cucumber, chopped herbs, and pine kernels into the bulgar wheat. Gently stir in the roasted tomatoes and any juices from the roasting tin. Chill in the refrigerator for 30 minutes. Adjust the seasoning to taste and serve garnished with the parsley sprigs.

SERVES 4

- 350 g/12 oz small vine-ripened tomatoes, halved
- 2 garlic cloves, finely chopped
- 1 tsp sugar
- 1 tsp sea salt flakes
- 4 tbsp extra virgin olive oil
- 200 g/7 oz bulgar wheat
- 2 tbsp white wine vinegar
- 85 g/3 oz cucumber, peeled and diced
- 2 tbsp chopped fresh flat-leaf parsley
- 2 tbsp chopped fresh mint
- 2 tbsp pine kernels, lightly toasted
- salt and pepper
- fresh flat-leaf parsley sprigs, to garnish

TABBOULEH

Put the quinoa into a medium-sized saucepan and cover with the water. Bring to the boil, then reduce the heat, cover and simmer over a low heat for 15 minutes. Drain if necessary.

Leave the quinoa to cool slightly before combining with the remaining ingredients in a salad bowl. Adjust the seasoning to taste before serving.

SERVES 4

175 g/6 oz quinoa

600 ml/1 pint water

10 vine-ripened cherry tomatoes, deseeded and halved

7.5-cm/3-inch piece cucumber, diced

3 spring onions, finely chopped

juice of ½ lemon

2 tbsp extra virgin olive oil

4 tbsp chopped fresh mint

4 tbsp chopped fresh coriander

4 tbsp chopped fresh flat-leaf parsley

salt and pepper

QUINOA SALAD WITH SUN-DRIED TOMATOES

SERVES 4

235 g/8½ oz quinoa

500 ml/18 fl oz water

10 sun-dried tomatoes (in oil, drained)

50 g/1¾ oz feta cheese, crumbled

2 spring onions, white parts, chopped

20 g/¾ oz mixed fresh herbs (basil, flat-leaf parsley, coriander), chopped

50 g/1¾ oz stoned black olives, chopped

dressing

5 tbsp roasted tomato oil

3 tbsp fresh lemon juice

1 garlic clove, crushed

salt and pepper

Put the quinoa into a medium-sized saucepan and cover with the water. Bring to the boil, then reduce the heat, cover and simmer over a low heat for 15 minutes. Drain if necessary. Rinse the grains thoroughly in a fine-mesh sieve and drain.

In a medium saucepan, bring the water to the boil over a high heat, stir in the quinoa and return to the boil. Lower the heat, cover, and simmer for about 15 minutes or until all the liquid has been absorbed. Remove from the heat, fluff up the quinoa with a fork and transfer to a bowl. Leave to cool a little.

Leave the quinoa to cool slightly before combining with the remaining ingredients in a salad bowl. Whisk the dressing ingredients together, pour over the quinoa, toss and serve.

SUCCATASH SALAD

SERVES 4–6

- 1 tbsp cider vinegar
- 1 tsp wholegrain mustard
- 1 tsp sugar
- 3 tbsp garlic-flavoured olive oil
- 1 tbsp sunflower oil
- 400 g/14 oz canned sweetcorn kernels, rinsed and drained
- 400 g/14 oz runner beans, finely chopped
- 2 peeled red peppers from a jar, drained and finely chopped
- 2 spring onions, finely chopped
- salt and pepper
- chopped fresh flat-leaf parsley, to garnish

Beat the vinegar, mustard and sugar together. Gradually whisk in the olive and sunflower oils to form an emulsion.

Stir in the sweetcorn kernels, runner beans, red peppers and spring onions. Add salt and pepper to taste and stir together again. Cover and chill for up to one day until required.

When ready to serve, adjust the seasoning, if necessary, and garnish with the parsley.

RED PEPPER & RADICCHIO SALAD

Core and deseed the peppers and cut into rounds.

Arrange the radicchio leaves in a salad bowl. Add the pepper, beetroot, radishes and spring onions. Drizzle with the dressing and serve with crusty bread.

SERVES 4

2 red peppers

1 head radicchio, separated into leaves

4 cooked whole beetroot, cut into matchsticks

12 radishes, sliced

4 spring onions, finely chopped

4 tbsp basic salad dressing

fresh crusty bread, to serve

WATERCRESS, COURGETTE & MINT SALAD

SERVES 4

2 courgettes, cut into batons

100 g/3½ oz French beans, cut into thirds

1 green pepper, deseeded and cut into strips

2 celery sticks, sliced

1 bunch watercress

dressing

200 ml/7 fl oz natural yogurt

1 garlic clove, crushed

2 tbsp chopped fresh mint

pepper

Bring a large saucepan of water to the boil, add the courgette batons and beans and cook for 5 minutes, or until just tender. Remove with a slotted spoon and refresh the beans under cold running water. Set aside to cool completely.

Mix the courgettes and beans with the pepper strips, celery and watercress in a large serving bowl.

To make the dressing, combine the yogurt, garlic and mint in a small bowl. Season with pepper to taste.

Spoon the dressing on to the salad and serve immediately.

CHICKPEA & TOMATO SALAD

If using dried chickpeas, soak overnight then boil for at least 30 minutes until soft. Leave to cool.

To make the dressing, put all the ingredients into a small screw-top jar and shake until well blended. Taste and add more lemon juice or oil if necessary.

Add the tomatoes, onion and basil to the chickpeas and mix gently. Pour over the dressing and mix again. Arrange on a bed of lettuce and serve with crusty bread.

SERVES 4

175 g/6 oz dried chickpeas or 400 g/14 oz canned chickpeas, drained and rinsed

225 g/8 oz ripe tomatoes, roughly chopped

1 red onion, thinly sliced

handful fresh basil leaves, torn

1 cos or romaine lettuce, torn

fresh crusty bread, to serve

dressing

1 green chilli, deseeded and finely chopped

1 clove garlic, crushed

juice and zest of 2 lemons

2 tbsp olive oil

1 tbsp water

pepper

MINTED PEA & RUNNER BEAN RICE SALAD

To make the dressing, put all the ingredients in a bowl and whisk together well.

Cook the rice in a saucepan of lightly salted boiling water for 10–12 minutes or until just tender. Drain well and transfer to a large serving bowl. Stir in the dressing and leave to cool.

Cook the runner beans, mangetout and peas in a saucepan of boiling water for 2 minutes. Drain well and refresh under cold running water. Stir into the rice. Adjust the seasoning to taste and serve garnished with the mint leaves.

SERVES 6

- 175 g/6 oz easy-cook long grain rice
- 140 g/5 oz runner beans, trimmed and diagonally sliced
- 85 g/3 oz mangetout, thinly sliced
- 115 g/4 oz frozen peas
- few fresh mint leaves, to garnish

dressing

- 4 spring onions, finely chopped
- 4 tbsp sunflower oil
- 2 tbsp white wine vinegar
- ½ tsp Dijon mustard
- 2 tbsp finely chopped fresh mint
- salt and pepper

THREE BEAN SALAD

SERVES 4–6

175 g/6 oz mixed salad leaves, such as spinach, rocket and curly endive

1 red onion

85 g/3 oz radishes

175 g/6 oz cherry tomatoes

115 g/4 oz cooked beetroot

280 g/10 oz canned cannellini beans, drained and rinsed

200 g/7 oz canned red kidney beans, drained and rinsed

300 g/10½ oz canned flageolet beans, drained and rinsed

40 g/1½ oz dried cranberries

55 g/2 oz roasted cashew nuts

225 g/8 oz feta cheese (drained weight), crumbled

dressing

4 tbsp extra virgin olive oil

1 tsp Dijon mustard

2 tbsp lemon juice

1 tbsp chopped fresh coriander

salt and pepper

Arrange the salad leaves in a salad bowl and reserve.

Thinly slice the onion, then cut in half to form half moons and put into a bowl.

Thinly slice the radishes, cut the tomatoes in half and peel the beetroot, if necessary, and dice. Add to the onion with the remaining ingredients, except the nuts and cheese. To make the dressing, put all the ingredients into a screw-top jar and shake until well blended. Pour over the bean mixture, toss lightly, then spoon on top of the salad leaves.

Scatter over the nuts and cheese and serve immediately.

SOYA BEAN & MUSHROOM SALAD

Steam the soya beans in a steamer or metal colander set over a pan of simmering water for 5–6 minutes until just tender. Rinse with cold water, drain well and transfer to a serving bowl. Add the mushrooms, spinach and rocket leaves and gently toss together.

To make the dressing, place all the ingredients in a bowl and whisk together. Pour the dressing over the salad and toss well to mix. Serve immediately with extra pepper.

SERVES 2

200 g/7 oz fresh soya (edamame) beans

55 g/2 oz closed-cup mushrooms, sliced

55 g/2 oz baby spinach leaves

handful of rocket leaves

dressing

3 tbsp light olive oil

1½ tbsp lemon juice

½ tsp Dijon mustard

1 tbsp snipped fresh chives

1 tbsp chopped fresh flat-leaf parsley

salt and pepper

FRUITY COTTAGE CHEESE SALAD

SERVES 4

85 g/3 oz cottage cheese

1 tsp chopped fresh flat-leaf parsley

1 tbsp snipped fresh chives

1 tsp chopped fresh chervil or basil

2 assorted coloured peppers, deseeded and peeled

1 small melon, such as Ogen (about 300 g/10½ oz after peeling and deseeding)

175 g/6 oz mixed salad leaves

55 g/2 oz seedless red grapes

1 red onion, thinly sliced

dressing

3 tbsp freshly squeezed lime juice

1 small fresh red chilli, deseeded and finely chopped

1 tsp clear honey

1 tbsp soy sauce

Place the cottage cheese in a bowl and stir in the chopped herbs. Cover lightly and reserve.

Cut the peeled peppers into thin strips and reserve. Cut the melon in half, discard the seeds and cut into small wedges.

Arrange the salad leaves on a large serving platter with the melon wedges.

Spoon the herb-flavoured cottage cheese on the platter and arrange the reserved peppers, grapes and red onion slices around the cheese.

To make the dressing, mix the lime juice, chilli, honey and soy sauce together in a small bowl. Drizzle over the salad and serve.

INDONESIAN WARM SALAD

SERVES 4

- 8 outer leaves of cos lettuce or similar dark, crisp lettuce leaves
- 100 g/3½ oz French beans, lightly cooked
- 100 g/3½ oz baby carrots, lightly cooked
- 250 g/9 oz new potatoes, cooked until just tender
- 1 tbsp groundnut oil
- 125 g/4½ oz fresh beansprouts
- 8-cm/3¼-inch piece cucumber, deseeded and cut into 4-cm/1½-inch batons
- 4 eggs, hard-boiled
- 1 small onion, sliced into rings

sauce

- 4 tbsp canned reduced-fat coconut milk
- 3 tbsp sugar-free smooth peanut butter
- juice of ½ lime
- 2 tsp light soy sauce
- dash of Tabasco sauce or any chilli sauce

Roughly tear the lettuce leaves, if large, and arrange on 4 individual serving plates. Halve the beans and cut the carrots, as necessary, into batons. Arrange these with the potatoes (cut into chunks if large) on the plates.

Heat the oil in a non-stick frying pan or wok over a high heat, add the beansprouts and stir-fry for 2 minutes until lightly cooked but still crisp. Remove with a slotted spoon and sprinkle over the cooked vegetables with the cucumber. Peel and quarter the eggs, then arrange on top of the salad.

Add the onion rings to the oil remaining in the frying pan or wok and stir-fry over a high heat for 5 minutes, or until golden and crisp. To make the sauce, combine all the ingredients in a bowl and pour over the salad. Top with the onion rings and serve immediately.

VEGETABLE & RICE NOODLE SALAD

To make the dressing, whisk all the ingredients together in a small bowl. Place the noodles in a shallow bowl, pour over boiling water and leave to soak for 5 minutes. Drain well and refresh under cold running water. Transfer to a salad bowl, pour over half the salad dressing and toss well.

Heat the sesame oil in a wok and stir-fry the garlic and ginger for 1 minute. Add the sweetcorn, broccoli, mangetout and pepper and stir-fry over a high heat for 2–3 minutes.

Add the hot vegetables to the noodles with the rest of the salad dressing and toss together. Cool, then stir in the beansprouts. Serve garnished with coriander leaves and chilli pepper.

SERVES 2

125 g/4½ oz rice noodles

2 tsp toasted sesame oil

1 garlic clove, crushed

1 tsp fresh ginger, grated

55 g/2 oz baby sweetcorn, thinly sliced

55 g/2 oz tiny broccoli florets

55 g/2 oz mangetout, thinly sliced

½ red pepper, deseeded and thinly sliced

85 g/3 oz beansprouts

fresh coriander leaves and chopped red chilli pepper, to garnish

dressing

2 tbsp peanut oil

1½ tbsp lime juice

2 tbsp sweet chilli sauce

salt and pepper

WARM ORIENTAL-STYLE SALAD

SERVES 4

115 g/4 oz broccoli florets

115 g/4 oz baby carrots, scraped and cut in half lengthways

140 g/5 oz pak choi

2 sprays sunflower oil

1 red onion, sliced

1–2 fresh bird's eye chillies, deseeded and sliced

2.5-cm/1-inch fresh ginger, grated

2 whole star anise

1 red pepper, deseeded and cut into strips

1 orange pepper, deseeded and cut into strips

115 g/4 oz baby courgettes, trimmed and sliced diagonally

115 g/4 oz baby sweetcorn, sliced in half lengthways

2 tbsp orange juice

1 tbsp soy sauce

1 tbsp cashew nuts

Cut the broccoli into tiny florets then bring a small saucepan of water to the boil and add the halved carrots. Cook for 3 minutes then add the broccoli and cook for a further 2 minutes. Drain and plunge into cold water then drain again and reserve.

Arrange 25 g/1 oz of pak choi on a large serving platter. Shred the remainder and set aside.

Heat a wok and when hot, add the oil and heat for 30 seconds. Add the sliced onion, chillies, ginger and star anise and stir-fry for 1 minute. Add the pepper strips, courgettes and baby sweetcorn and stir-fry for a further 2 minutes.

Pour in the orange juice and soy sauce and continue to stir-fry for a further 1 minute before adding the reserved shredded pak choi, broccoli and carrots. Stir-fry for 2 minutes, or until the vegetables are tender but still firm to the bite. Arrange the warm salad on the pak choi-lined serving platter, scatter the cashew nuts over the top and serve.

CHICKEN & SPINACH SALAD

SERVES 4

3 celery sticks, thinly sliced

½ cucumber, thinly sliced

2 spring onions, thinly sliced

250 g/9 oz young spinach leaves

3 tbsp chopped fresh flat-leaf parsley

350 g/12 oz boneless, roast chicken, sliced thinly

smoked almonds, to garnish

dressing

2.5-cm/1-inch piece of fresh ginger, grated finely

3 tbsp olive oil

1 tbsp white wine vinegar

1 tbsp clear honey

½ tsp ground cinnamon

salt and pepper

Toss the celery, cucumber and spring onions in a large bowl with the spinach leaves and parsley.

Transfer the salad to serving plates and arrange the chicken on top.

To make the dressing, put all the ingredients into a small screw-top jar and shake until well blended. Pour the dressing over the salad. Garnish with a few smoked almonds.

THAI-STYLE CHICKEN SALAD

SERVES 4

- 400 g/14 oz new potatoes, halved lengthways
- 200 g/7 oz baby sweetcorn
- 150 g/5½ oz beansprouts
- 3 spring onions, trimmed and sliced
- 4 cooked, skinless chicken breasts, sliced
- 1 tbsp chopped lemon grass
- 2 tbsp chopped fresh coriander
- salt and pepper
- wedges of lime and fresh coriander leaves, to garnish

dressing

- 6 tbsp chilli oil or sesame oil
- 2 tbsp lime juice
- 1 tbsp light soy sauce
- 1 tbsp chopped fresh coriander
- 1 small red chilli, deseeded and finely sliced

Bring two saucepans of water to the boil. Put the potatoes in one saucepan and cover with cold water. Bring to the boil, cover and simmer for 15 minutes, or until tender when pierced with a fork. Put the baby sweetcorn into the other saucepan and cook for 5 minutes until tender. Drain the potatoes and baby sweetcorn well and leave to cool.

When the vegetables are cool, transfer them into a large serving dish. Add the beansprouts, spring onions, chicken, lemon grass and coriander and season with salt and pepper.

To make the dressing, put all the ingredients into a screw-top jar and shake well. Drizzle the dressing over the salad and garnish with lime wedges and coriander leaves. Serve immediately.

TURKEY SALAD PITTAS

Preheat the grill to high.

Put the spinach leaves, red pepper, carrot and hummus into a large bowl and stir together, so all the salad ingredients are coated with the hummus. Stir in the turkey and sunflower seeds and season with salt and pepper to taste.

Put the pitta bread under the grill for about 1 minute on each side to warm through, but do not brown. Cut it in half to make 2 'pockets' of bread.

Divide the salad between the bread pockets and serve.

MAKES 2

small handful baby leaf spinach, rinsed, patted dry and shredded

½ red pepper, deseeded and thinly sliced

½ carrot, peeled and roughly grated

4 tbsp hummus

85 g/3 oz boneless, skinless cooked turkey meat, thinly sliced

½ tbsp toasted sunflower seeds

1 wholemeal pitta bread

salt and pepper

TUNA & AVOCADO SALAD

SERVES 4

- 2 avocados, stoned, peeled and cubed
- 250 g/9 oz cherry tomatoes, halved
- 2 red peppers, deseeded and chopped
- handful fresh flat-leaf parsley
- 2 garlic cloves, crushed
- 1 fresh red chilli, deseeded and finely chopped
- juice of ½ lemon
- 6 tbsp olive oil
- 3 tbsp sesame seeds
- 4 fresh tuna steaks, about 150 g/5½ oz each
- 8 cooked new potatoes, cubed
- fresh rocket leaves and fresh crusty bread, to serve
- pepper

Toss the avocados, tomatoes, red peppers, parsley, garlic, chilli, lemon juice and 2 tablespoons of the oil together in a large bowl. Season to taste with pepper, cover and chill in the refrigerator for 30 minutes.

Lightly crush the sesame seeds in a mortar with a pestle. Tip the crushed seeds on to a plate and spread out. Press each tuna steak in turn into the crushed seeds to coat on both sides.

Heat 2 tablespoons of the remaining oil in a frying pan, add the potatoes and cook, stirring frequently, for 5–8 minutes, or until crisp and brown. Remove from the pan and drain on kitchen paper.

Wipe out the pan, add the remaining oil and heat over a high heat until very hot. Add the tuna steaks and cook for 3–4 minutes on each side.

To serve, divide the avocado salad between 4 serving plates. Top each with a tuna steak, scatter over the potatoes and rocket leaves and serve with crusty bread.

TUNA WITH BEANSPROUT SALAD

Mix the soy sauce, oil and ginger in a shallow dish. Add the tuna steaks and turn to coat in the marinade. Cover and leave to marinate for 1 hour at room temperature.

Heat a cast iron griddle pan until very hot. Drain the tuna steaks from the marinade and place in the hot pan. Cook for 2 minutes then turn over and cook for a further 1–2 minutes until the steaks are well seared but still a little pink in the middle. Cook for a further 2–3 minutes if you prefer the tuna well done.

To make the dressing, place all the ingredients in a small pan and heat gently, stirring, until just warmed through.

Mix the alfalfa sprouts, beansprouts and mustard and cress in a bowl and toss together with the lime juice. Season with salt and pepper.

Divide the sprouting salad between 4 serving plates and top with the tuna steaks. Drizzle over the warm dressing. Garnish with lime wedges and serve immediately.

SERVES 4

2 tbsp soy sauce
1 tbsp sunflower oil
1 tsp fresh ginger, grated
4 tuna steaks, about 175 g/6 oz each
55 g/2 oz fresh alfalfa sprouts
55 g/2 oz fresh beansprouts
25 g/1 oz mustard and cress
squeeze of lime or lemon juice
salt and pepper
lime wedges, to garnish

dressing

3 tbsp sunflower oil
2 tbsp soy sauce
1 tbsp clear honey
2 tbsp rice vinegar

SALT CHILLI SQUID SALAD

To make the dressing, mix all the ingredients together in a bowl to taste, cover and refrigerate until required.

Cut the squid tubes into 5-cm/2-inch pieces, then score diamond patterns lightly across the flesh with the tip of a sharp knife. Heat the oil in a wok or large frying pan over a high heat, add the squid pieces and tentacles and stir-fry for 1 minute. Add the chillies and spring onions and stir-fry for a further minute. Season to taste with salt and pepper and add a good squeeze of lemon juice.

Mix the watercress and spinach together, then toss with enough of the dressing to coat lightly. Serve immediately with the squid, together with the lemon wedges to squeeze over the squid.

SERVES 4

12 squid tubes and tentacles (about 700 g/1 lb 9 oz total weight), cleaned and prepared

2–3 tbsp olive oil

1–2 red chillies, deseeded and thinly sliced

2 spring onions, finely chopped

lemon wedges, for squeezing and to serve

3 good handfuls watercress

2 handfuls baby spinach or rocket

salt and pepper

dressing

100 ml/3½ fl oz olive oil

juice of 1 lime

1 tsp caster sugar

2 shallots, thinly sliced

1 tomato, peeled, deseeded and finely chopped

1 garlic clove, crushed

SPICY WARM CRAB SALAD

SERVES 4

- 2 sprays sunflower oil
- 1 fresh serrano chilli, deseeded and finely chopped
- 115 g/4 oz mangetout, cut in half diagonally
- 6 spring onions, trimmed and finely shredded
- 25 g/1 oz frozen sweetcorn kernels defrosted
- 150 g/5½ oz white crabmeat, drained if canned
- 55 g/2 oz raw prawns, peeled and deveined, thawed if frozen
- 1 carrot, about 85 g/ 3 oz, peeled and grated
- 115 g/4 oz beansprouts
- 225 g/8 oz fresh baby spinach leaves
- 1 tbsp finely grated orange rind
- 2 tbsp orange juice
- chopped fresh coriander, to garnish

Heat a wok and when hot, spray in the oil and heat for 30 seconds. Add the chilli and mangetout then stir-fry over a medium heat for 2 minutes.

Add the spring onions and sweetcorn and continue to stir-fry for a further 1 minute.

Add the crabmeat, prawns, grated carrot, beansprouts and spinach leaves. Stir in the orange rind and juice and stir-fry for 2–3 minutes, or until the spinach has begun to wilt and everything is cooked. Serve divided between 4 bowls, sprinkled with the chopped coriander.

FRUIT

CHILLED BERRY BREAKFAST SALAD

Place all the berries in a shallow bowl. Stir in the orange juice and sugar. Cover and chill in the refrigerator for at least 2 hours or overnight.

Put the yogurt in a small bowl and fold in the orange rind and honey.

Divide the chilled salad between 4 serving bowls. Top each with a dollop of the yogurt and sprinkle with the sunflower seeds and hazelnuts. Serve immediately.

SERVES 4

- 225 g/8 oz small strawberries, halved
- 140 g/5 oz raspberries
- 115 g/4 oz blackberries
- 115 g/4 oz blueberries
- juice and finely grated rind of 1 orange
- 1 tbsp caster sugar
- 6 tbsp Greek yogurt
- 1 tbsp orange blossom honey
- 1 tbsp sunflower seeds
- 1 tbsp toasted chopped hazelnuts

GREEN FRUIT SALAD

SERVES 4

1 honeydew melon

2 green apples

2 kiwi fruit

125 g/4½ oz seedless green grapes

fresh mint sprigs, to decorate

syrup dressing

1 lemon

150 ml/5 fl oz white wine

150 ml/5 fl oz water

4 tbsp clear honey

few sprigs of fresh mint

To make the syrup dressing, pare the rind from the lemon using a potato peeler.

Put the lemon rind in a saucepan with the white wine, water and clear honey. Bring to the boil, then simmer gently for 10 minutes.

Remove the syrup from the heat. Add the sprigs of mint and leave to cool.

To prepare the fruit, first cut the melon in half and scoop out the seeds. Use a melon baller or a teaspoon to make melon balls.

Core and chop the apples. Peel and slice the kiwi fruit.

Strain the cooled syrup into a serving bowl, removing and reserving the lemon rind and discarding the mint sprigs.

Add the apple, kiwi fruit, grapes and melon to the serving bowl. Stir through gently to mix.

Serve the fruit salad, decorated with sprigs of fresh mint and some of the reserved lemon rind.

TROPICAL FRUIT SALAD

SERVES 4

1 papaya

1 mango

1 pineapple

4 oranges, peeled and cut into segments

125 g/4½ oz strawberries, hulled and quartered

single or double cream, to serve (optional)

syrup dressing

6 tbsp caster sugar

400 ml/14 fl oz water

½ tsp ground mixed spice

grated rind of ½ lemon

To make the syrup dressing, put the sugar, water, mixed spice and lemon rind into a saucepan. Bring to the boil, stirring continuously, then continue to boil for 1 minute. Remove from the heat and leave to cool to room temperature. Transfer to a jug or bowl, cover with clingfilm and chill in the refrigerator for at least 1 hour.

Peel and halve the papaya and remove the seeds. Cut the flesh into small chunks or slices, and put into a large bowl. Cut the mango twice lengthways, close to the stone. Remove and discard the stone. Peel and cut the flesh into small chunks or slices, and add to the bowl. Cut off the top and bottom of the pineapple and remove the hard skin. Cut the pineapple in half lengthways, then into quarters, and remove the tough core. Cut the remaining flesh into small pieces and add to the bowl. Add the orange segments and strawberries.

Pour over the chilled syrup, cover with clingfilm and chill until required. Serve with single or double cream, if using.

EXOTIC FRUIT COCKTAIL

SERVES 6

2 oranges

2 large passion fruit

1 pineapple

1 pomegranate

1 banana

Cut 1 orange in half and squeeze the juice into a bowl, discarding any pips. Using a sharp knife, cut away all the peel and pith from the second orange. Working over the bowl to catch the juice, carefully cut the orange segments between the membranes to obtain skinless segments of fruit. Discard any pips.

Cut the passion fruit in half, scoop the flesh into a nylon sieve and, using a spoon, push the pulp and juice into the bowl of orange segments. Discard the pips.

Using a sharp knife, cut away all the skin from the pineapple and cut the flesh lengthways into quarters. Cut away the central hard core. Cut the flesh into chunks and add to the orange and passion fruit mixture. Cover and refrigerate the fruit at this stage if you are not serving immediately.

Cut the pomegranate into quarters and, using your fingers or a teaspoon, remove the red seeds from the membrane. Cover and refrigerate until ready to serve – do not add too early to the fruit cocktail as the seeds discolour the other fruit.

Just before serving, peel and slice the banana, add to the fruit cocktail with the pomegranate seeds and mix thoroughly. Serve immediately.

PAPAYA SALAD

To make the dressing, whisk together the oil, Thai fish sauce, lime juice, sugar and chilli. Set aside, stirring occasionally to dissolve the sugar.

Shred the lettuce and white cabbage, then toss together and arrange on a large serving plate.

Peel the papayas and slice them in half. Scoop out the seeds, then slice the flesh thinly. Arrange on top of the lettuce and cabbage.

Soak the tomatoes in a bowl of boiling water for 1 minute, then lift out and peel. Remove the seeds and chop the flesh. Arrange on the salad leaves.

Scatter the peanuts and spring onions over the top. Whisk the dressing and pour over the salad. Garnish with basil leaves and serve at once.

SERVES 4

1 crisp lettuce

1/4 small white cabbage

2 papayas

2 tomatoes

25 g/1 oz roasted peanuts, chopped roughly

4 spring onions, trimmed and sliced thinly

fresh basil leaves, to garnish

dressing

4 tbsp olive oil

1 tbsp Thai fish sauce or light soy sauce

2 tbsp lime or lemon juice

1 tbsp dark muscovado sugar

1 tsp finely chopped fresh red or green chilli

MOROCCAN ORANGE SALAD

SERVES 4

- 5 large oranges
- 1 small red onion, finely sliced
- ½ tsp ground cumin
- ½ tsp ground coriander
- 1 tbsp roughly chopped fresh flat-leaf parsley
- 1 tbsp roughly chopped fresh coriander
- salt and pepper

Using a serrated knife cut away the peel and all the white pith from 4 of the oranges. Cut the flesh into thin slices removing any pips. Place the orange slices in a shallow dish with the onion.

Halve and squeeze the juice from the remaining orange. Mix the juice with the cumin and coriander and pour over the orange slices. Cover and chill in the refrigerator for 1 hour.

Add the parsley and coriander to the orange slices and mix gently. Pile onto a serving dish and season lightly with salt and pepper before serving.

FENNEL & ORANGE SALAD

SERVES 4

2 oranges, peeled and sliced

1 bulb Florence fennel, thinly sliced

1 red onion, peeled and sliced into thin rings

dressing

juice of 1 orange

2 tbsp balsamic vinegar

pepper

Arrange the orange slices in the bottom of a shallow dish. Place a layer of fennel on top and then add a layer of onion.

To make the dressing, mix the orange juice with the vinegar and drizzle over the salad. Season with pepper and serve.

MELON & MANGO SALAD

To make the melon dressing, whisk together the yogurt, honey and ginger in a small bowl.

Halve the melon, scoop out the seeds with a spoon and discard. Slice, peel and dice the flesh. Place in a bowl with the grapes.

Slice the mango on each side of its large flat stone. On each mango half, slash the flesh into a criss-cross pattern, down to but not through the skin. Push the skin from underneath to turn the mango halves inside out. Now remove the flesh and add to the melon mixture.

Arrange the watercress and lettuce leaves on 4 serving plates.

To make the salad leaves dressing, whisk together the olive oil and vinegar with a little salt and pepper. Drizzle over the salad leaves.

Divide the melon mixture between the 4 plates and spoon over the melon dressing.

Scoop the seeds out of the passion fruit and sprinkle them over the salads. Serve immediately or chill in the refrigerator until required.

SERVES 4

1 cantaloupe melon

55 g/2 oz seedless red grapes, halved

55 g/2 oz seedless green grapes

1 large mango

1 bunch watercress, trimmed

handful iceberg lettuce leaves, shredded

1 passion fruit

melon dressing

150 ml/5 fl oz natural yogurt

1 tbsp clear honey

1 tsp fresh ginger, grated

salad leaves dressing

2 tbsp olive oil

1 tbsp cider vinegar

salt and pepper

MELON & STRAWBERRY SALAD

SERVES 4

½ iceberg lettuce, shredded

1 small honeydew melon

225 g/8 oz strawberries, sliced

5-cm/2-inch piece cucumber, thinly sliced

fresh mint sprigs, to garnish

dressing

200 g/7 fl oz natural yogurt

5-cm/2-inch piece cucumber, peeled

a few fresh mint leaves

½ tsp finely grated lime or lemon rind

pinch of caster sugar

3–4 ice cubes

Arrange the shredded lettuce on 4 serving plates.

Cut the melon lengthways into quarters. Scoop out the seeds and cut through the flesh down to the skin at 2.5-cm/1-inch intervals. Cut the melon close to the skin and detach the flesh.

Place the chunks of melon on the beds of lettuce with the strawberries and cucumber slices.

To make the dressing, put the yogurt, cucumber, mint leaves, lime rind, caster sugar and ice cubes into a blender or food processor. Blend together for about 15 seconds until smooth.

Serve the salad with a little dressing poured over. Garnish with sprigs of fresh mint.

MINTED PEA & MELON SALAD

Cut all the melon flesh into even-sized chunks removing any seeds. Place the chunks in a bowl with the cucumber.

To make the dressing, place all the ingredients in a small bowl and whisk together.

Pour the dressing over the melon and cucumber and toss well to coat. Cover and chill for 1 hour.

Add the pea shoots to the chilled melon and cucumber and gently toss together. Transfer to a serving bowl and serve garnished with mint leaves.

SERVES 4

350 g/12 oz wedge of watermelon

½ small honeydew melon

½ Charentais or cantaloupe melon

½ cucumber, peeled and diced

55 g/2 oz fresh pea shoots

fresh mint leaves, to garnish

dressing

3 tbsp light olive oil

1 tbsp white wine vinegar

½ tsp caster sugar

1 tbsp chopped fresh mint

salt and pepper

PROSCIUTTO WITH MELON & ASPARAGUS

SERVES 4

225 g/8 oz asparagus spears

1 small or ½ medium-sized Galia or cantaloupe melon

55 g/2 oz prosciutto, thinly sliced

150 g/5½ oz mixed salad leaves, such as herb salad with rocket

85 g/3 oz fresh raspberries

1 tbsp freshly shaved prosciutto

salt

dressing

1 tbsp balsamic vinegar

2 tbsp raspberry vinegar

2 tbsp orange juice

Trim the asparagus, cutting in half if very long. Cook in lightly salted, boiling water over a medium heat for 5 minutes, or until tender. Drain and plunge into cold water then drain again and reserve.

Cut the melon in half and scoop out the seeds. Cut into small wedges and cut away the rind. Separate the prosciutto slices, cut in half and wrap around the melon wedges.

Arrange the salad leaves on a large serving platter and place the melon wedges on top together with the asparagus spears.

Scatter over the raspberries and Parmesan shavings. To make the dressing, put all the ingredients into a small screw-top jar and shake until well blended. Pour over the salad and serve.

CANTALOUPE & CRAB SALAD

SERVES 4

350 g/12 oz fresh crabmeat

5 tbsp mayonnaise

50 ml/2 fl oz natural yogurt

4 tsp extra virgin olive oil

4 tsp lime juice

1 spring onion, finely chopped

4 tsp finely chopped fresh flat-leaf parsley

pinch of cayenne pepper

1 cantaloupe melon

2 radicchio heads, separated into leaves

flat-leaf fresh parsley sprigs, to garnish

fresh crusty bread, to serve

Place the crabmeat in a large bowl and pick over it very carefully to remove any remaining shell or cartilage, but try not to break the meat up.

Place the mayonnaise, yogurt, olive oil, lime juice, spring onion, chopped parsley and cayenne pepper into a separate bowl and mix until thoroughly blended. Fold in the crabmeat.

Cut the melon in half and remove and discard the seeds. Slice into wedges, then cut off the rind with a sharp knife.

Arrange the melon wedges and radicchio leaves in 4 serving bowls, then arrange the crabmeat mixture on top. Garnish with a few sprigs of fresh parsley and serve with crusty bread.

FIG & WATERMELON SALAD

Cut the watermelon into quarters and scoop out and discard the seeds. Cut the flesh away from the rind, then chop the flesh into 2.5-cm/1-inch cubes. Place the watermelon cubes in a bowl with the grapes. Cut each fig lengthways into 8 wedges and add to the bowl.

To make the syrup dressing, grate the lime and mix the rind with the orange rind and juice, maple syrup and honey in a small saucepan. Bring to the boil over a low heat. Pour the mixture over the fruit and stir. Leave to cool. Stir again, cover and chill in the refrigerator for at least 1 hour, stirring occasionally.

Divide the fruit salad equally between 4 bowls and serve.

SERVES 4

1 watermelon, weighing about 1.5 kg/3 lb 5 oz

115 g/4 oz seedless red grapes

4 figs

syrup dressing

1 lime

grated rind and juice of 1 orange

1 tbsp maple syrup

2 tbsp clear honey

SPRING CLEAN SALAD

Core and dice the apples, place in a bowl and pour over the lemon juice. Mix well to prevent discoloration.

Add the rest of the fruit and vegetables to the bowl and mix gently. Pour in the walnut oil, mix again and serve.

SERVES 4

2 dessert apples, cored and diced

juice of 1 lemon

large chunk of watermelon, deseeded and cubed

1 head chicory, sliced into rounds

4 sticks celery with leaves, roughly chopped

1 tbsp walnut oil

RASPBERRY & FETA SALAD

SERVES 6

350 g/12 oz couscous

600 ml/1 pint boiling chicken stock or vegetable stock

350 g/12 oz fresh raspberries

small bunch of fresh basil

225 g/8 oz feta cheese, cubed or crumbled

2 courgettes, thinly sliced

4 spring onions, trimmed and diagonally sliced

55 g/2 oz pine kernels, toasted

grated rind of 1 lemon

dressing

1 tbsp white wine vinegar

1 tbsp balsamic vinegar

4 tbsp extra virgin olive oil

juice of 1 lemon

salt and pepper

Put the couscous in a large, heatproof bowl and pour over the stock. Stir well, cover and leave to soak until all the stock has been absorbed.

Pick over the raspberries, discarding any that are overripe. Shred the basil leaves.

Transfer the couscous to a large serving bowl and stir well to break up any lumps. Add the cheese, courgettes, spring onions, raspberries and pine kernels. Stir in the basil and lemon rind and gently toss all the ingredients together.

To make the dressing, put all the ingredients into a small screw-top jar and shake until well blended. Pour over the salad and serve.

STRAWBERRY & WATERCRESS SALAD

To make the balsamic glaze, place the vinegar and sugar in a small saucepan. Heat gently, stirring, until the sugar dissolves. Simmer gently for 5–6 minutes until syrupy. Cool for 30 minutes.

Place the watercress in a serving dish. Scatter over the strawberries. Halve, stone, peel and slice the avocado and toss gently in the lemon juice. Add to the salad. Scatter over the cucumber and walnuts.

Drizzle the glaze over the salad. Season lightly with salt and pepper and serve immediately.

SERVES 4

115 g/4 oz watercress, tough stalks removed

350 g/12 oz strawberries, sliced

1 ripe avocado

1 tbsp lemon juice

¼ cucumber, finely diced

1 tbsp chopped walnuts

salt and pepper

balsamic glaze

100 ml/3½ fl oz balsamic vinegar

2 tbsp sugar

FETA, MINT & STRAWBERRY SALAD

To make the dressing, mix the vinegar, sugar, mustard and salt together in a bowl until smooth. Slowly pour in the oil, whisking constantly.

Bring a large saucepan of water to the boil, add the beans and cook for 5 minutes, or until just tender. Remove with a slotted spoon and refresh the beans under cold running water. Hull and halve the strawberries, then add to the beans. Stir in the pistachio nuts and mint leaves. Toss the salad with enough of the dressing to coat lightly.

Break the feta cheese into chunks and scatter over the salad. Add a good grinding of pepper and serve immediately.

SERVES 4–6

500 g/1 lb 2 oz French beans

500 g/1 lb 2 oz strawberries

2–3 tbsp pistachio nuts

1 small bunch fresh mint leaves

500 g/1 lb 2 oz feta cheese (drained weight)

pepper

dressing

2 tbsp raspberry vinegar

2 tsp caster sugar

1 tbsp Dijon mustard

pinch of salt

125 ml/4 fl oz olive oil

WARM PEACH & GOAT'S CHEESE SALAD

SERVES 4

- 4 just ripe peaches, halved, stoned and cut into 6 slices
- 1 tbsp olive oil
- 2 tsp lemon juice
- 55 g/2 oz lamb's lettuce
- 55 g/2 oz curly endive
- 125 g/4½ oz mild goat's cheese, crumbled
- 4 slices Serrano ham
- 1 tbsp toasted hazelnuts, chopped

dressing

- 4 tbsp olive oil
- 2 tbsp hazelnut oil
- 2 tbsp red wine vinegar
- ½ tsp sugar
- salt and pepper

To make the dressing, place all the ingredients in a small bowl and whisk together well.

Place the peach slices in a bowl and add the olive oil and lemon juice. Turn to coat and season lightly with salt and pepper.

Heat a cast iron griddle pan and add the peach slices. Cook over a medium heat for 2–3 minutes, turning once, until lightly charred and just starting to soften.

Mix the lamb's lettuce and curly endive together in a bowl and add half the dressing. Toss well to coat and divide between 4 serving plates. Top with the warm peach slices and crumbled goat's cheese. Place a ruffled slice of ham on the top of each salad.

Drizzle over the rest of the dressing and scatter over the toasted hazelnuts. Serve immediately.

PEAR & ROQUEFORT SALAD

To make the dressing, place the cheese in a bowl and mash with a fork. Gradually blend the yogurt into the cheese to make a smooth dressing. Add the chives and season with pepper to taste.

Tear the lollo rosso, radicchio and lamb's lettuce leaves into manageable pieces. Arrange the salad leaves on a large serving platter or divide them between individual serving plates.

Cut the pears into quarters and remove the cores. Cut the quarters into slices. Arrange the pear slices over the salad leaves.

Drizzle the dressing over the pears and garnish with a few whole chives.

SERVES 4

few leaves of lollo rosso

few leaves of radicchio

few leaves of lamb's lettuce

2 ripe pears

whole fresh chives, to garnish

dressing

55 g/2 oz Roquefort cheese

150 ml/5 fl oz natural yogurt

2 tbsp snipped fresh chives

pepper

PEAR & STILTON SALAD

SERVES 4

250 g/9 oz dried orecchiette pasta

1 head radicchio, torn into pieces

1 oakleaf lettuce, torn into pieces

2 pears

1 tbsp lemon juice

250 g/9 oz Stilton cheese, diced

55 g/2 oz chopped walnuts

4 tomatoes, quartered

55 g/2 oz canned sweetcorn

1 red onion, sliced

1 carrot, grated

8 fresh basil leaves

55 g/2 oz lamb's lettuce

dressing

4 tbsp olive oil

2 tbsp lemon juice

1 tbsp white wine vinegar

salt and pepper

Bring a large, heavy-based saucepan of lightly salted water to the boil. Add the pasta, return to the boil and cook for 8–10 minutes, or until tender but still firm to the bite. Drain, refresh in a bowl of cold water and drain again.

Place the radicchio and oakleaf lettuce leaves in a salad bowl. Halve the pears, remove the cores and dice the flesh. Toss the diced pear with the lemon juice in a small bowl to prevent discoloration. Top the salad with the Stilton, walnuts, pears, pasta, tomatoes, sweetcorn, onion slices and grated carrot. Add the basil and lamb's lettuce.

To make the dressing, mix the olive oil, lemon juice and vinegar together in a bowl, then season to taste with salt and pepper. Pour the dressing over the salad, toss and serve.

BEANSPROUT, APRICOT & ALMOND SALAD

SERVES 4

115 g/4 oz beansprouts

small bunch seedless red and green grapes, halved

12 unsulphured dried apricots, halved

25 g/1 oz blanched almonds, halved

pepper

dressing

1 tbsp walnut oil

1 tsp sesame oil

2 tsp balsamic vinegar

Place the beansprouts in the bottom of a large salad bowl and sprinkle the grapes and apricots on top.

To make the dressing, put all the ingredients into a small screw-top jar and shake until well blended. Pour over the salad.

Scatter over the almonds and season.

CHICKEN & GRAPEFRUIT SALAD

Place the chicken in a large saucepan and pour over enough water to cover. Add the bouquet garni and peppercorns and bring to a gentle simmer. Cover and simmer for 25–30 minutes until just cooked through. Leave the chicken to cool in the liquid.

Using a serrated knife, cut away the peel and pith from the grapefruit. Holding the fruit over a bowl to catch any juice, segment the flesh. Reserve 2 tablespoons of the juice.

Toss the salad leaves in a bowl with the grapefruit segments.

To make the dressing, place all the ingredients in a small bowl with the reserved grapefruit juice. Whisk together until thoroughly blended.

Drain the poached chicken and pat dry with kitchen paper. Tear into bite-sized strips or thinly slice. Arrange on top of the salad. Drizzle over the dressing and garnish with chervil sprigs.

SERVES 4

- 2 skinless, boneless chicken breasts, about 175 g/6 oz each
- 1 bouquet garni
- few black peppercorns
- 2 pink grapefruit
- 3 Little Gem lettuces, separated into leaves
- 1 head chicory, separated into leaves
- fresh chervil sprigs, to garnish

dressing

- 1 tbsp light olive oil
- 3 tbsp Greek yogurt
- 1 tsp wholegrain mustard
- pinch of sugar
- 1 tbsp chopped fresh chervil
- salt and pepper

CHICKEN & CRANBERRY SALAD

Carve the chicken carefully, slicing the white meat. Divide the legs into thighs and drumsticks and trim the wings. Cover with clingfilm and refrigerate.

Put the cranberries in a bowl. Stir in the apple juice, cover with clingfilm and leave to soak for 30 minutes.

Meanwhile, blanch the mangetout, refresh under cold running water and drain.

Separate the lettuce hearts and arrange on a large serving platter with the avocados, mangetout, watercress, rocket and the chicken.

To make the dressing, put all the ingredients into a small screw-top jar and shake until well blended.

Drain the cranberries and mix them with the dressing, then pour over the salad. Serve immediately.

SERVES 4

1 smoked chicken, weighing 1.3 kg/3 lb

115 g/4 oz dried cranberries

2 tbsp apple juice or water

200 g/7 oz mangetout

4 lettuce hearts

2 ripe avocados, peeled, stoned and sliced

1 bunch watercress, trimmed

55 g/2 oz rocket

dressing

2 tbsp olive oil

1 tbsp walnut oil

2 tbsp lemon juice

1 tbsp chopped fresh mixed herbs, such as parsley and lemon thyme

salt and pepper

PRAWNS WITH PINEAPPLE & PAPAYA SALSA

SERVES 8

4 tbsp sunflower oil

1 fresh red chilli, deseeded and chopped

1 garlic clove, crushed

48 prawns

chopped fresh flat-leaf parsley, to garnish

pineapple & papaya salsa

1 large papaya, halved, deseeded, peeled and cut into 5-mm/ ¼-inch dice

1 small pineapple, halved, cored, peeled and cut into 5-mm/ ¼-inch dice

2 spring onions, very finely chopped

1 red chilli, or to taste, deseeded and finely chopped

1 garlic clove, very finely chopped

2½ tsp lemon juice

½ tsp ground cumin

¼ tsp salt

pepper

To make the pineapple and papaya salsa, put the papaya in a large bowl with the pineapple, spring onions, chilli, garlic, lemon juice, cumin, salt and pepper. Adjust the lemon juice, cumin, salt or pepper to taste, if necessary. Cover and chill until required, ideally at least 2 hours.

Heat a wok over a high heat. Add the oil and swirl around, then add the chilli and garlic and stir-fry for 20 seconds. Add the prawns and stir-fry for 2–3 minutes until the prawns are cooked through, become pink and curl.

Tip the prawns, garlic and any oil left in the wok into a heatproof bowl and leave the prawns to cool and marinate in the chilli oil. When the prawns are completely cool, cover the bowl and chill for at least 2 hours.

When ready to serve, give the salsa a stir and adjust the seasoning, if necessary. Arrange a mound of salsa on each of 8 plates. Remove the prawns from the marinade and divide between plates. Sprinkle with parsley and serve.

INDEX